NUMB3RS THAT

PROPHESY

Troy Brewer's book *Numbers That Prophesy* proves undoubtedly that Troy is brilliant. Only a very remarkable mind could think through these numbers in a way to see events through such a lens. Numbers are not my specialty, but I found this book so riveting that I read it from cover to cover in a single sitting. As I finished each chapter totally amazed, I quickly started the next one with anticipation to see what I would find next. If you love prophecy—and if you enjoy biblical typology and biblical numerology and how they can relate to past and future events—you will find this book captivating. Wow!

Rick Renner
Minister, Author, Broadcaster
Moscow, Russia

Numbers That Prophesy by my friend Troy Brewer is a profound and eye-opening journey into the prophetic significance of numbers in Scripture. Troy masterfully reveals how God speaks through numbers to guide, encourage, reveal, and confirm His purposes. This book is a must-read for anyone looking to understand the hidden messages of God's numerical language in scripture. It will deepen your faith and sharpen your spiritual discernment and prophetic understanding. I highly recommend it for those seeking fresh revelation of divine truth and vision.

Patricia King
Founder of Patricia King Ministries

We are living in extraordinary times, and it is crucial, now more than ever, to hear what the Spirit of God is saying to the church (Revelation 3:22). In his new book, Troy Brewer presents a compelling investigation into prophetic "parables" found in world-shaking news stories from the past two centuries. By applying a prophetic lens to a macro view of world history, he illuminates messages from the heart of God that have timely takeaways for our lives today. *Numbers That Prophesy* is a biblically sound and prophetically attuned book that will help you to be like "the sons of Issachar" and rightly discern our God-given assignments for this pivotal season (1 Chronicles 12:32).

Dr. Ché Ahn
Senior Leader, Harvest Rock Church, Pasadena, CA
President, Harvest International Ministry
International Chancellor, Wagner University

Troy Brewer's must-read book will empower you to discern prophetic seasons, sequences, and patterns found in numbers. Learn to encounter God's voice every day and everywhere, and get ready to fill journals with the profound revelations Jesus will unveil to you!

Darren Stott
Pastor of Eden Church, Founder of Supernaturalist Ministries, and CEO of Renaissance Coalition

DESTINY IMAGE BOOKS BY TROY A. BREWER

*Redeeming Your Timeline: Supernatural Skillsets
for Healing Past Wounds, Calming Future Anxieties,
and Discovering Rest in the Now*

*Looking Up (Updated & Expanded Edition): Understanding Prophetic
Signs in the Constellations and How the Heavens
Declare the Glory of God*

*40 Breakthrough Declarations: Powerful Prayers to Heal Past Hurts,
Make Future Provision, and Invite Jesus into Your Timeline*

*Numbers that Prophesy: Hearing God Through Historic Headlines
and Numbers That Preach*

NUMB3RS THAT
PROPHESY
HEARING GOD THROUGH HISTORIC
HEADLINES AND NUMBERS THAT PREACH
TROY A. BREWER
FOREWORD BY JOSEPH Z

DESTINY IMAGE® PUBLISHERS, INC.
P.O. Box 310, Shippensburg, PA 17257-0310
"Publishing cutting-edge prophetic resources to supernaturally empower the body of Christ"

This book and all other Destiny Image and Destiny Image Fiction books are available at Christian bookstores and distributors worldwide.

For more information on foreign distributors, call 717-532-3040.
Reach us on the Internet: www.destinyimage.com.

ISBN 13 TP: 978-0-7684-8288-1
ISBN 13 eBook: 978-0-7684-8289-8

For Worldwide Distribution, Printed in the U.S.A.
1 2 3 4 5 6 7 8 / 28 27 26 25 24

DEDICATION

I dedicate this book to my one wife, Leanna.

To our four children: Maegan, Ben, Luke, and Rhema.

To my seven grandchildren: Barrett, Sophia, Evelyn, Branch, Annabell, Paula Jayne, Jeremiah, and August. There may be more in the future to whom I also dedicate this book, but haven't had the pleasure to love on, yet.

And to the spouses of our children: Patrick, JC, Brandi, and Madi. Each of you are an answered prayer.

Saying I thank God for you and love you isn't enough, but it's all I can do on this page.

My dedication of this book to you means all the hard work, laughter, and joy I present with this work is done in your honor because you mean so much to me.

Heritage, legacy, and the passing of the "Jesus torch" are what we steward, and our greatest honor is in loving each other in the Kingdom.

Love to you all,

Me

Numbers By Design

Note from the Designer

In creating this book cover, we set out to develop something that worships King Jesus through its design, as well as its look and feel. There are millions of book covers out there, but for *Numbers That Prophesy,* we needed to match the revelation within the book with the details of the cover. Below, you will find a working list of the details in the design, including numbers, placements, sequences, dates, and more, that have been prayerfully added to give this book cover a prophetic edge over anything the world can offer.

There are a total of 107 layers, in reference to the Columbia space shuttle crew of the STS-107.

Both the front and back covers are designed using the Golden Ratio, the rule of thirds, and the Fibonacci Sequence. You will notice this as a common theme as we walk through.

- The Golden Ratio is a mathematical ratio created by God, and most often found in nature. It signifies God's hand in all of the designs.

- The rule of thirds and the Fibonacci sequence are used as a certain order that many of the assets are aligned to.

The front cover contains the moon on the top, placed using the Golden Ratio, speaking to God's message for Israel. The back cover's Golden Ratio is the front cover inverted. You'll notice the sun placed in the opposite spot, addressing God's message for humanity.

THE FRONT COVER

- At 222x222px in the top left corner, you'll notice the code made of 1's and 0's changes to 222, signifying the miracle working power of God even at work in the digital space today (Acts 2:22).

- At the top, you'll see a mirrored image of Abraham Lincoln embedded in the moon, showing how history repeats itself and that we should not only look to it, but learn from it.

- The number 47 sits between the shoulder of President Lincoln and the chilling waters of the Titanic's resting place. This is representative of Isaiah 47, which speaks of the judgment of God. This number is prophetically placed at a strategic intersection in the golden Ratio.

- The width of the book title's text area is 1776px in reference to our nation's birthday.

THE BACK COVER

- The number 28 is placed behind Princess Diana and Mother Teresa as an example of the times and seasons, and it is exactly 107px beneath "History's Headlines."

- Pastor Troy's right eye is at pixel number 1966 from the top (his birth year).

- His right ear is at the 126th pixel mark signifying the day he was born. This is in reference to the priest's ability to hear the Word of the Lord and declare it to His people.

THE SPINE

- The number 8 (new beginnings) is printed on the spine and duplicated 28 times in reference to Luke 11:28 and Joel 2:28, as a reminder to both keep His Word and receive the promise of an outpouring.

CONTENTS

Foreword   xvi

Introduction: God's Prophetic Word Throughout the Ages
and Modern Events   1

1   Prophetic Historic Event 1: President Lincoln and the
Civil War   27

2   Prophetic Historic Event 2: The RMS Titanic   45

3   Prophetic Historic Event 3: "Man" on the Moon   97

4   Prophetic Historic Event 4: The Space Shuttle Columbia   121

5   Prophetic Historic Event 5: Princess Diana and
Mother Teresa   145

6   Prophetic Historic Event 6: 9/11 Terrorist Attack on
the United States of America   169

7   The Hype of Type   185

Last Words   220

Addendum   221

Numbers That Preach and Their Meaning   221

Dream Interpretation Guide   249

About the Author   275

FOREWORD

God is always speaking. The question is, are you listening? An even more significant question is whether you can perceive His voice and fingerprints by observing our natural world.

Many years ago, when seeking the Lord about visions and dreams, I asked the Lord, "Why do You conceal what You are speaking in types, dreams, symbols, signs, and the like? Why don't You say it plainly to us? That question led me to the passage in John 16, where the disciples had similar thoughts regarding Jesus's use of parabolic language. The disciples struggled to grasp what Jesus was telling them until He plainly explained His relationship with the Father. In response, they exclaimed, "Now we understand you because you are speaking plainly!" Jesus's reply was interesting. He answered by saying, "Do you now believe?" Suggesting that although He was verbally writing in crayon for them, they still were not fully persuaded because, in the following verses, He told them they would be scattered, which suggests their enthusiasm for His simplified clarity would not be enough to carry them through.

A day came when the Holy Spirit ministered a word to me in my search for clarity and simplification as I asked Him why all the signs, parables, and unique ways of navigating His voice, and He answered me with this: *"Because I want to be pursued."* What a word! God speaks in these veiled ways because He desires a relationship and to be pursued! Imagine that! God, the creator of the universe, wants to be pursued!

There are few who understand the dynamic of pursuing God better than my friend Troy Brewer. He is not just a highly prophetic individual but a son of Issachar with an uncanny ability. Troy approaches the voice of God like a giant game tracker, at ease in his element while far off the conventional beaten path. He has a Holy Spirit sense to see things every day and discern the signs of our times through identifying the tapestry of God's handiwork in current events and by recognizing the numerical significance in many historical scenarios that have and continue to shape this generation.

Among the many things I admire about Troy is his bold defiance of evil as he enters hellish situations and brings liberty through the clarity of God's voice. He exemplifies a man who walks in revelation, and any man who walks in a revelation from God is not at the mercy of a culture going mad.

This book is an invitation to interpret the world around you. Troy walks in the office of the prophet and, as such, builds up the Kingdom of God, tears down the kingdom of darkness, and calls the people of God into action. He is anointed to speak to current and cultural issues in real time. True to the office of the prophet and much like Daniel 5:12, Troy's book *Numbers That Prophesy* offers an avenue of operating in knowledge, understanding, interpreting dreams, solving riddles, and explaining enigmas!

Troy Brewer is one of the most unique voices and cause-driven men of God I have ever met. His work to rescue children, pastor a successful church, and stand as a leading voice in the prophetic is truly exceptional. My respect for him and the impact he has made on this generation goes far beyond his tremendous insights in this book. Thank you, Troy, for your inspiring work!

Joseph Z
Author, Broadcaster, Prophetic Voice
JosephZ.com

GOD'S PROPHETIC WORD THROUGHOUT THE AGES AND MODERN EVENTS

Attention all dreamers: God is prophetically speaking dream language through the common and epic events of the headlines that get your attention.

Most people think that prophecy is foresight. Biblically, a big part of the prophetic is a prophetic lens of what's going on around you at the moment. It is also the prophetic picture of hindsight. We see this throughout the New Testament in examples such as when Peter stood up and said, "This is THAT which was spoken of by the prophet Isaiah 700 years ago." He was saying, "This is what Isaiah was saying prophetically, and now you're seeing the picture of it today."

Hindsight prophetic, or prophetic from a rearview mirror, is not something that's really respected or even thought about, and this book is meant to be a conversation starter.

Once you start to look at the prophetic this way, you will seek God in a deep way. It is important to ask what word our God was speaking through these modern events. Then, hopefully, we can begin to partner with Holy Spirit and ask, "What is God speaking through my circumstances going on around me?" As I look at this event in my past, or the history of my family, or the history of my people, I ask, what was the word of God in *that* and how is it relevant to me today? Because all of it, the past, present, and future, are prophetic.

In the Throne Room of Heaven, we witness a vivid illustration of the prophetic. That's exactly what the seraphim around the throne do. They prophesy, "Holy is the Lord God Almighty who *was*, and who *is*, and who is *yet to come*. They're prophesying the amazing things God has done through past prophetic, current prophetic, and future prophetic. And that's greatly needed in the body of Jesus.

The Bible specifically says they have eyes behind them, beside them, and in front of them. Every single time they circle the throne, they see something glorious that God did, something glorious that God is doing, and something glorious that God is going to do.

Our spiritual eyes must be open to see what He has said and see what that means for us today. When John was on the Isle of Patmos, he received the Revelation of Jesus Christ. He wrote, *"Then I turned to see the voice that spoke with me"* (Revelation 1:12 NKJV).

How do we "see" a voice? We look at what God did around us. He had the Gospel writers tell us we have the Savior who knows and understands what it is like to live as a human on earth by showing us Jesus as He walked here. We heard about His compassion by the way He healed and redeemed the people. We heard about His obedience to do hard things when we saw Him sweating drops of blood as He sought the Father before His crucifixion. We see the hope we have because He rose and walked again, as witnessed by more than 500 people. We heard these things so we can know how to live as His followers, filled with compassion, obedience, prevailing prayer, and hope in our world today.

Jesus is not just a historical figure, He is the central theme of biblical prophecy. The book of Revelation unveils the "more" about Him. He reigns on the throne in Heaven, overseeing the unfolding of history. We see Him as the slain Lamb, our sacrificial offering, now alive and reigning as the King. We see Him as a Warrior who will return soon to judge His enemies and restore His world. Finally, we see Him as the Bridegroom, ready to unite with His church for eternity.

As we await that day, His prophetic voice is speaking all around us. It reminds us of what God has done in the past; it tells us what He is doing right now and what He will do in the coming days to tighten our grip on our faith in Him. We have a future and a hope built on these things. In everything He does, His voice gives us clarity, instruction, and wisdom, and that voice carries forth in the tone of His never-ending love for us and His desire for our well-being.

As history is being written, in between the lines, you can find the interpretation of the sign and a word from God Himself. A word that could be the difference between life and death.

Warning words in the headlines are just like warning dreams, and you go back to sleep at your own peril.

If you learned this to be true, it would change how you look at the top stories of your news feed and how you review your history book.

God is speaking to all of us right now using words from historical events from long ago.

What if I told you God is prophetically speaking not just through history but through everything going on around you personally as an individual? I mean, actually speaking to you through the things going on with you in your life.

He is.

God is speaking through everything going on around you!

I will show you how if you continue reading.

What if I told you God was prophetically speaking to each generation through the pop culture of all we as a society engage in?

Yes, He is. Furthermore, He always has.

If you know anything about the book of Revelation, you know what Jesus said to the church of Laodicea. The message that Jesus had for the church in Laodicea is as relevant today as it was 2,000 years ago.

But did you know that Jesus was prophetically interpreting an event in their local "headlines"?

JESUS IN THE HEADLINES

Apparently, the church had grown "lukewarm" in their faith and zeal for Jesus. To drive the point home, Jesus used a word-picture that the local citizens understood well from a recent and current event in their cultural headlines.

> *I know your works, that you are neither cold nor hot. I could wish you were cold or hot. So then, because you are lukewarm, and neither cold nor hot, I will vomit you out of My mouth* (Revelation 3:15-16 NKJV).

In the day Jesus spoke these words to the church, ancient Laodicea was marketed to the Roman Empire as the new vacation spot and the first city in the world to boast of having hot and cold running water. A brilliant Roman aqueduct system piped in hot spring water from the south and cold spring water from nearby Colossae, the opposite direction.

On what you and I might refer to as "the ribbon-cutting day," a high Roman official arrived and took his first ceremonial drink with all the pomp and pageantry you expect.

To the shame of everyone in charge and the citizens who had moved there, he dramatically spit it out and declared it made him want to throw up! The water had been moved by water bridges, as pipes wouldn't be around for hundreds of years, and by the time the water arrived in Laodicea, it was the same temperature as the air.

So here we have an easy-to-identify biblical record of Jesus using the top news feed story as a prophetic picture to speak to the church in that era. The Word that Jesus spoke to that church 2,000 years ago still speaks to the church today. Do you know why? Because we are part of the same Church that those people were part of 2,000 years ago.

You and I, together, no matter our denomination, race, or geographical location, are part of the same church that Peter, James, and John were part of. The Word is good for all of us.

God is revealing deep revelation knowledge through the common cultural events of every society on earth, and I will do my best to prove it throughout the content of this book.

We are going to look at the Bible and our history through the same lens because the Author of both is the same.

The Language of Dreams Through Everyday Experiences

If you are living a victorious Kingdom life, your value for His voice is high. You hear through the little happenings and also through the big events—through everything in which you are involved. Because you know His Word, you recognize His voice through subtle and major activities during your life and day.

The more mature you are, and the more you lean into His engagement, the more you gain interpretation, revelation, and application of what God is revealing to you, just like in your dream life.

You spend two-thirds of your life awake and one-third of your life asleep. Both belong to the Lord, and His prophetic language of symbols, numbers, type, shadows, and parables is His intimate way of powerfully communicating to you in a very personal way.

More than 20 years ago, I heard Graham Cooke and Dave Crone say, "Everything in the Kingdom is relational before it is functional." This truth changed my life, and I started paying attention to how Heaven invades my earth in the daytime and during the night—and I found out very quickly it's the same relational language.

A long time ago, when my oldest son was only about 5 years old, it snowed a rare, heavy snow in North Central Texas. I was walking across my small front yard, and when I looked behind me, I saw that Ben was jumping from one of my tracks to the next track.

"Daddy, I'm going to walk where you walk," he said with a big grin.

The fear of the Lord came on me, and it hit me so powerfully that I started to tear up.

If that were a dream, what would it mean?

It didn't take a next-level prophet to interpret what God was showing me through this little personal moment. My beautiful little boy was going to follow me, not through my tracks in the mud, but through my tracks in the snow.

> *"Come now, let us settle the matter," says the Lord. "Though your sins are like scarlet, they shall be as white as snow..."* (Isaiah 1:18 NIV).

Today, Ben is in his 30s and has kids of his own. He did indeed follow me into a walk with King Jesus. He also helped me launch my radio ministry and works in all of my media. He recently preached his first message at OpenDoor Church.

It wasn't a dream; it was a personal event in my everyday life. It prophetically came true.

It's similar to when God spoke to the prophet Jeremiah and began to instruct him that his prophetic voice was in the common things going on around him. He just had to see it.

> *Moreover the word of the Lord came to me, saying, "Jeremiah, what do you see?" And I said, "I see a branch of an almond tree." Then the Lord said to me, "You have seen well, for I am ready to perform My word." And the word of the Lord came to me the second time, saying, "What do you see?" And I said, "I see a boiling pot, and it is facing away from the north"* (Jeremiah 1:11-13 NKJV).

What?! God is speaking through a pot of boiling water? Has God ever spoken to you through your teatime or coffee break?

I bet He has, even if you don't know it. I am sure that He will if you are willing to consecrate your normal living space to His extraordinary presence.

Once you see His hidden voice in the common things around you, you can't unsee it.

I have also heard the voice of God through thunderous and epic events in my life. I'm sure you have as well.

Oh, there was the time God gave me a church campus on the same exact calendar day as I had experienced a terrible church split just two years prior. *And* it was flag day: "The Lord is our banner."

> *And Moses built an altar and called its name, The-Lord-Is-My-Banner* (Exodus 17:15 NKJV).

> *We will rejoice in your salvation, and in the name of our God we will set up our banners! May the Lord fulfill all your petitions* (Psalm 20:5 NKJV).

> *You have given a banner to those who fear You, that it may be displayed because of the truth. Selah* (Psalm 60:4 NKJV).

And the numbers of the new church location were the same as the numbers of the address of our last location. We moved from 301 S. Main Street, Joshua, Texas, to 301 S. Dobson, Burleson, Texas.

I will extol You, O Lord, for You have lifted me up, and have not let my foes rejoice over me (Psalm 30:1 NKJV).

And it was exactly 7.7 miles from the front door of one building to the front door of the new building.

Seventy-seven is the number of the church. The word *church* is in the Bible 77 times. The term "house of God" is in the Bible 77 times.

See, I knew all that and was able to recognize it because I live my life looking for the word that testifies of Jesus. If I had dreamed it, I would have known what it meant. Then, when I live it, I can understand what it means. That's the privilege of His children who know His voice and seek out the matter.

Jesus rebuked the leaders of His day because they missed such things.

And in the morning, "it will be foul weather today, for the sky is red and threatening." Hypocrites! You know how to discern the face of the sky, but you cannot discern the signs of the times (Matthew 16:3 NKJV).

I don't want to miss it.

God's timeless truth can be seen by looking at historic events through a biblically prophetic lens. As long as there have been headlines, God has wanted the people reading or experiencing them to see the event from His point of view—and there is no excuse for not catching it.

Prophetic people know that. The rest of the world does not, yet God continues to speak to everybody through what is going on around them.

> For ever since the creation of the world His invisible attributes, His eternal power and divine nature, have been clearly seen, being understood through His workmanship [all His creation, the wonderful things that He has made], so that they [who fail to believe and trust in Him] are without excuse and without defense (Romans 1:20 AMP).

My friend, there is a clear Kingdom message in the midst of every worldly event. There is a definitive Word from God to all people throughout history, which He amplifies through thunderous events. But just because God is speaking doesn't mean people know it. And just because a few know it does not mean they understand it.

You have to interpret the event, the names, and the numbers that prophesy. You have to learn the language of the prophetic.

HISTORY OF *NUMBERS THAT PREACH*

In 1996, just months after Leanna and I founded OpenDoor Church, I bought my first home computer on Black Friday from Walmart. At 5 a.m., I carted a giant PC to my little pickup truck, and later that afternoon, I plugged into America Online through our dial-up phone connection.

The next year, after learning to surf the web and peck out word processing, I began to collect all my notes and draft a book titled *Numbers That Preach*.

I put it together the best I could. I self-published it through a good man with a tiny company in California. I handed it out at my little church and made it available through my first website, and, well, that's about it.

My interest in how God speaks through numbers was not shared by very many peers. It was considered too close to New Age and witch-craft beliefs at that time. The subject matter was strange to the very few people I tried to introduce it to, and there was really no reason for anyone to consider me an authority on anything. They were right. Besides that, it wasn't like I had a marketing plan or anything.

So, *Numbers That Preach* sat on my shelf year after year, and I really just thought it was something God had me do for me and for a few people around me.

Then, in 2015, I was invited to appear on my very first TV show, and it was a big one—"Dreams and Mysteries" with John Paul Jackson. John Paul had passed away the year before, and Steve and Ginny Maddox were producing new seasons with guest speakers. My good friend Byron Easterling introduced us, and before I knew it I was in his world-famous studios near Dallas.

Oh, I was excited and nervous, but God was with me, and Steve asked me back to do five shows in all. The first show on The Mystery of Numbers came out in 2016, and my book started flying off the shelf.

It had been laying there dormant for nearly two decades, and now we couldn't print enough books to keep up with the worldwide demand. I was astonished!

When the Arecibo message is broken into 73 groups of 23 characters (both prime numbers) and each group read from right to left, it forms this graphic. The real message of course contained no color information; colors are used here to identify sections of the message.

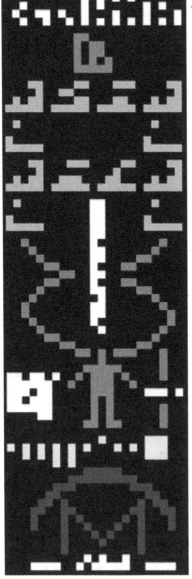

<--Right to left, the numbers 1 to 10;

<--Atomic numbers of hydrogen, carbon, nitrogen, oxygen and phosphorus, the basic chemicals of life on earth

<--Formulas for the chemical building blocks of DNA

<--A representation of the DNA double helix; in white, the number of nucleotides in the human genome

<--A stick figure of a human being, tied into the DNA helix; at the left, the population of Earth (about 4 billion at the time of the message); at the right, the typical height of a human, 5' 9.5", in units of the wavelength of the transmission; below, a schematic of our solar system, with the third planet raised toward the human figure

<--Drawing of the Arecibo radio telescope; below, a number representing the diameter of the dish

Source: https://news.cornell.edu/stories/1999/11/25th-anniversary-first-attempt-phone-et-0

People had been seeing 11-11 everywhere and 222. Why were there 153 fish in the biblical net, and why were they having dreams with 153? I was flooded with cards, letters, and emails about encounters people were having with Jesus at 1:11 and 3:33 in the morning.

Suddenly, my book became required reading in seminaries, and though I had never attended university, I was being asked to speak at them.

Marcus and Joni Lamb invited me to Daystar, Ward Simpson invited me to GodTV, and by the time Covid hit, churches around the world were talking about and acknowledging the prophetic language of numbers. It's not the numbers people need to see, but the Word of God that the numbers point to.

I really had little to do with it, I was just caught up in a wave of a move of God. I had the right language at a place where the light came on and the veil came off. I think there have been much better works written on the subject. Some of my favorites are E.W. Bullinger and Michael Hoggard. *Numbers That Preach* has held its own in the hearts of prophetic people everywhere though. I can't tell you the joy this has given me.

It is not an "American thing," it's a Kingdom thing. I have had the honor of visiting and preaching in 56 nations, and God is getting everyone's attention through His amazing prophetic language of numbers and how things are measured.

Now that we are learning to hear it, I believe God is taking the lid off of the revelation of the hidden narratives and prophetic declarations through the events of thunderous historic events.

God has been speaking throughout our timelines, and it is now time for us to hear and heed what He has spoken.

He has designed the symbols of math to speak to every language on earth. Numbers actually prophesy. In the case of NASA, they believe math is the language we can use to speak to other worlds. The smartest people among us understand that the prophetic pictures in numbers are actually universal.

THE UNIVERSAL LANGUAGE OF NUMBERS

Numbers are the artistic science of sending a deliberate message to an audience who doesn't speak your language.

On a humid day back in 1974, a group of world-famous scientists gathered in Puerto Rico for a top-secret ceremony. They didn't let the world know because they knew the message would be criticized by every agenda in humanity. So, they pointed Arecibo Observatory's giant radio telescope toward a cluster of 300,000 stars and ramped up the transmitter to more than a million watts of power. Pushing a single button, they sent the world's first deliberate message to anyone listening in outer space.

The date was 11/16.

Traveling at the speed of light, this postcard from Earth blasted through our atmosphere past the waves from brand-new powerful FM radio stations. A million watts of radio signal cut through the songs of Elton John, Lynyrd Skynyrd, John Denver, and Aretha Franklin on a 25,000-year journey to reach its target.

Carl Sagan and other notable scientists of the day decided this message should be about 3 minutes long. It had what they described as "vital information" about our species, including a crude stick-figure representation of a human, a DNA double helix, atomic numbers of the chemicals necessary for life on Earth, and a drawing of a telescope.

It was basically a secret radio signal inviting any intelligent civilization, good or bad, who came across it to come find us. A personal invitation to seek us out, dig deeper, and get to know us better.

Out-of-line crazy, you think? No. It's actually normal practice for any well-established NASA nerd to try to communicate with intelligent beings who might come across us.

This isn't the only time we have sent deliberate messages to intergalactic beings. In 1977, NASA launched the Voyager 1 and 2 spacecraft containing "artifacts" from Earth and flung them to parts unknown. The same invitation was given to anyone who happened to come across our little hunk of metal flying through the vastness of space. In essence, they were saying, "There's more to us than this. Come and seek us. If this got your attention, there is way more to be discovered about us. You are welcome here."

The equivalent of a message in a subatomic bottle being thrown into the Marianas Trench, it's not mathematically likely to be picked up by anything, even if it could be. It points to the sender's deliberate intention—the purpose—to convey an intended invitation, and they did it through numbers.

The Arecibo Message and the Voyager artifacts are just two of many examples of humans trying to communicate a deliberate message to an audience that doesn't speak our language—in this case, intended receivers in outer space and other galaxies. In every case, do you know how the smartest minds in the world communicated our message? Through numbers and symbols, just like how God speaks prophetically.

Why did they choose numbers and symbols as the voice of their message? Because they were trying to reach every language conceivable throughout the universe the only way they could—through numbers and symbols.

NUMBERS AND SYMBOLS

Amid the endless diversity of God's creation, He has designed a few things to have universal keys that unlock, well, everything! From the very beginning, God has used the precision of math and the symbol of numbers to communicate a deliberate message to those willing to seek Him. To the prophetic seeker of Jesus, letters and words are translated from numbers and math. Numbers prophesy just like the stars of Heaven.

> *The heavens declare the glory of God; and the firmament shows His handiwork. There is no speech nor language where their voice is not heard* (Psalm 19:1,3 NKJV).

Not only do words and math prophesy God's warnings and promises, the details of how the words are written and how the math is presented also prophesy.

> *For assuredly, I say to you, till heaven and earth pass away, one* **jot** *or one* **tittle** *will by no means pass from the law till all is fulfilled* (Matthew 5:18 NKJV).

Biblically, the prophetic message to the seeker is completely lost if they ignore the numbers and symbols intentionally given by the Holy Spirit. It's a lot like finding the Voyager 1 and 2 spacecraft, realizing the machine is not natural, and then missing the actual message from the sender because you refused to look at the numbers and symbols engraved on it. How ridiculous would that be?

Just like that, consider the actual message of the numbers and symbols that prophesy in the following biblical texts.

> *Now Enoch, the seventh from Adam, prophesied about these men also, saying, "Behold, the Lord comes with ten thousand of His saints"* (Jude 1:14 NKJV).

The 14th verse of the mysterious book of Jude tells us that Enoch was the 7th from Adam. So what? Is that supposed to mean something to us? Well, it obviously meant something to the Lord, or He would not have delivered that specific message for us to seek out.

Enoch wasn't the 6th generation from Adam, and he wasn't the 8th. He was the 7th. So, what is the Lord telling us about the number 7 and Enoch's place in the bloodline of Christ?

> *And Enoch walked with God; and he was not, for God took him* (Genesis 5:24 NKJV).

"Walking with God" implies both righteousness and relationship—things that qualified Enoch to prophetically see something at the very end of human time—the return of King Jesus Himself. The number 7 is about fulfillment, fullness, and completion. It represents the end of a timeline—a 7-day week—just as the number 8 represents a new beginning.

With that said, the one who saw the very end of days and the church coming back with the Lord on a white horse also saw the rapture of the church personally. Hebrews 11:5 tells us Enoch was *"taken away,"* so he did not see death at the ripe old age of 365. Other versions use *"translated"* or *"taken up"* rather than "taken away."

Wait a minute! That's the number of days in a Gregorian calendar year. The Jews don't even follow this solar calendar. They use a lunar calendar of 355 days. To the Western world and the Gentile people, this is where the beginning meets the end. Could there be a message in these numbers, and if so, who would that message be for?

God is very deliberate. The sender of the message intentionally placed a definite message there! But you have to seek it out.

> *It is the glory of God to conceal a matter, but the glory of kings*
> *is to search out a matter* (Proverbs 25:2 NKJV).

Enoch was the 7th from Adam and he prophesied about Jesus, whom Scripture shows was the 77th generation from Adam. So why all the 7s? What is God telling us about Enoch, Jesus, fullness, fulfillment, and the end of a timeline?

As mentioned previously, the word *church* is in the King James New Testament 77 times, as is the term "house of God." King Jesus is the Head of the church, which was birthed out of His death on the cross and resurrection 3 days later (another deliberate message). He is coming back for His church at the end of days and, like Enoch, His bride will be mysteriously whisked away. Do you see it?

> *For the Lord Himself will descend from heaven with a shout,*
> *with the voice of an archangel, and with the trumpet of God.*
> *And the dead in Christ will rise first. Then we who are alive*
> *and remain shall be caught up together with them in the clouds*
> *to meet the Lord in the air. And thus we shall always be with*
> *the Lord* (1 Thessalonians 4:16-17 NKJV).

We have to respect the fact that God gives us numbers that prophesy because He wants us to understand the message and the love behind it—not just be fascinated with the bottle the message comes in. Speaking of the 14th verse of Jude, which is 7+7, the following are some 14s that are prophetically woven into the story of Jesus.

> *So all the generations from Abraham to David are **fourteen** generations, from David until the captivity in Babylon are **fourteen** generations, and from the captivity in Babylon until the Christ are **fourteen** generations* (Matthew 1:17 NKJV).

The number 14 prophesies "generational promises." This is when God proves He will keep His covenant from one generation to the next generation. I would bet folded money that Matthew knew 14 has the numeric value of the name David. I think he tied all that together when he was bringing up the bloodline of the prophesied "Son of David." I have no idea if he knew the words "hand" and "gold" also have the numeric value of 14 in Hebrew gematria.

GEMATRIA: NUMERIC VALUE OF A WORD OR LETTER

What is gematria? It's a phenomenon that happens when a language also uses its letters as numbers. Just like the Greek and Roman languages, each letter in the Hebrew alphabet is also a number. Therefore, each word also adds up to a numeric value. That means every word—every verse and passage of your Bible—is also a number. Do you see how numbers can truly prophesy?

Note that we are *not* talking about numerology, which is the twisted belief that numbers actually give direction and power to those who live their lives based on them. That is what witches and New Age mystics do, just as they look to their horoscope as the "voice" of the universe directing them day in and day out. Let me tell you this—there is *no power in numbers.* None! God speaks through them, but we do not carve out a shrine and worship the messages in the numbers any more than we worship the numbers themselves.

That said, know this, too—there is the greatest power in God's Word. That's the starting point of this book you're reading—the numbers and symbols surrounding historic headlines prophesy a message from the God who uses everything to introduce Himself to a people who may or may not understand His message.

God is the Author and Inventor of all things numeric and mathematical. Numbers bring a depth of prophetic insight to each and every event and headline.

Continuing with the number 14, Passover begins on the fourteenth day of the Nisan. That is most likely the day Jesus was born and, positively, the day Jesus died on the Cross.

The "Torah of the Lord"—translated as "God, the Lord God"—is mentioned 14 times in the books of Chronicles (KJV). In the King James version of the Bible, the expression "the fear of the Lord" occurs 14 times in the book of Proverbs.

Israel became a nation again on the 14th day of May in 1948. I would say that qualifies for generational promises. I would also say there is a deliberate message in the timing (14) of this prophecy *fulfilled* at the *end of a timeline* (7+7).

THE VOICE WITHIN THE THUNDER—EPIC EVENTS AS PROPHETIC MARKERS

In the year that King Uzziah died, I saw the Lord... (Isaiah 6:1 NKJV).

Throughout the ages, the linear great halls of time have seen countless epic events that captivate the human imagination. The drama of all humankind's history has been produced from the hard choices people face, such as natural catastrophes, the theater of politics, the hope of love, the tragedy of terrible defeat, and the triumph of achieving victory.

Some of these events have made an impression—even an impact—across cultures, languages, and generations. The events are so dramatic they leave a mark on time itself.

Prophetic markers are spiritual indicators pointing to the promises and warnings of God's Word through real-time events. Like finding an "X" on an old pirate map, prophetic markers tell you exactly where to dig.

You have seen the shaking that these prophetic events made upon their generations, but have you heard the voice inside the thunder? Most people only see the epic event, but they do not hear the voice of the Lord within that event. This can be seen as Paul relates his conversion experience to an audience in Jerusalem:

And those who were with me indeed saw the light and were afraid, but they did not hear the voice of Him who spoke to me (Acts 22:9 NKJV).

Just like that, the voice of God was hidden within the account of the Titanic and Hindenburg disasters. It's a clear and definitive Word that God is still speaking today if you can respect the numbers that prophesy.

And 9/11 is not just a number. It's a date and a marker in time. The prophetic marker of 9/11 is also a message to us in these end days. It's part of our culture. It is God prophesying to anyone willing to hear His voice in the midst of the thunder. Most will not qualify, but that's not you. You will be committed to searching out the matter within the message.

> ...Then a voice came from heaven, saying, "I have both glorified it and will glorify it again." Therefore the people who stood by and heard it said that it had thundered. Others said, "An angel has spoken to Him." Jesus answered and said, "This voice did not come because of Me, but for your sake" (John 12:28-30 NKJV).

The Lord is speaking through the amazing headlines around us, and the prophetic markers are stamped upon our history. Together, we will discover the heart of the Father through the Word and the numeric voice within it. Once we learn how to tune in, we will never see the headlines without "turning to see the voice," as John did on the Isle of Patmos. We learn it through pursuing the joy and wonder of the Word, and by daring to look into the numbers that prophesy.

Welcome, my friend, to a front-row seat to human events as we discover the Voice within the thunder and the prophetic messages within some of history's greatest triumphs and tragedies.

Once you see it, you can't unsee it.

This is going to be fun.

Troy

Six Prophetic Legacies

Headlines grab the world's attention, capture the thoughts of those affected by them, and then often simply fade away. Some headlines, however, are so explosive that the events they call the world's attention to leave lasting legacies in the minds and hearts of people around the world.

Our search for numbers that prophesy will take us deeply into the details of 7 legacy-leaving stories. Our search is not to find details to amuse or mind-blowing connections through the numbers. Our search is to hear the voice of God and listen for His heartbeat echoing from these situations. Listen well to what He says because that word is still relevant today.

By searching out His messages from the prophetic hindsight of these stories, our spiritual hearing may be amplified so we don't miss anything He is saying to us today for the future. We will be better able to say, "Speak, Lord, for Your servant is listening."

"Simple laws can very well describe complex structures. The miracle is not the complexity of our world, but the simplicity of the equations describing that complexity."
—Sander Bais, Theoretical Physicist

"History is a vast early warning system."
—Norman Cousins, American Political Journalist

"There are symbolic dreams—dreams that symbolize some reality. Then there are symbolic realities—realities that symbolize a dream."
—Haruki Murakami, Japanese Writer
and Imaginative Translator

"History, despite its wrenching pain, cannot be unlived; but if faced with courage, need not be lived again."
—Maya Angelou, American Writer
and Civil Rights Activist

1

PROPHETIC HISTORIC EVENT 1

PRESIDENT LINCOLN AND THE CIVIL WAR

Source: https://www.loc.gov/resource/ppmsca.19301

I would bet a penny you have heard of President Lincoln's assassination, but have you heard of his prophetic dream? The dream tells us to look at the event as if it were a dream. It's staggering and a good place for Chapter 1.

If you look at the names, numbers, and circumstances of the 16th president's death as if a prophetic dream, you would have a word from God that could change your course and impact your destiny—the way Lincoln's life and death impacted the course and destiny of the United States of America.

PROPHETIC MESSAGE

ABRAHAM LINCOLN'S PROPHETIC DREAM

The week of his assignation, President Lincoln met with some close friends. Just two days earlier, General Lee had surrendered at Appomattox, and the Union had finally beaten the Confederacy. This dream happened a week before the official end of the war, and Lincoln would die 5 days after the end of the war.

According to Ward Hill Lamon, personal friend and self-appointed bodyguard to Lincoln, he heard the president share this dream with his wife and several friends just 3 days before His assassination:

> About ten days ago, I retired very late. I had been up waiting for important dispatches from the front. I could not have been long in bed when I fell into a slumber, for I was weary. I soon began to dream. There seemed to be a death-like stillness about me. Then I heard subdued sobs as if a number of people were weeping. I thought I left my bed and wandered downstairs. There, the silence was broken by the same pitiful sobbing, but the mourners were invisible.
>
> I went from room to room; no living person was in sight, but the same mournful sounds of distress met me as I passed along. I saw light in all the rooms; every object was familiar to me; but where were all the people who were grieving as if their hearts

would break? I was puzzled and alarmed. What could be the meaning of all this?

Determined to find the cause of a state of things so mysterious and so shocking, I kept on until I arrived at the East Room, which I entered. There I met with a sickening surprise. Before me was a catafalque, on which rested a corpse wrapped in funeral vestments. Around it were stationed soldiers who were acting as guards; and there was a throng of people, gazing mournfully upon the corpse, whose face was covered, others weeping pitifully. "Who is dead in the White House?" I demanded of one of the soldiers, "The President," was his answer, "he was killed by an assassin." Then came a loud burst of grief from the crowd, which woke me from my dream. I slept no more that night; and although it was only a dream, I have been strangely annoyed by it ever since.[1]

If you don't know about the prophetic dream ol' honest Abe had about his terrible demise, you might be reading this thinking, *Wow!* But there is a true historical record of such an event, and I think God gave it not just for our president, but for all prophetic people to consider throughout the ages to follow.

We are going to look at such events through a prophetic lens.

I think the 16th president's dream was the invitation for all prophetic people to learn to look at this happening with this important question in mind: *If the death of President Lincoln was a prophetic dream, what would it mean?*

Lincoln himself was a prophetic dreamer on more than one occasion.

A recurring dream that was a big prophetic marker for Lincoln was one in which he was on a ship moving rapidly through the water toward a vast and unknown shore. He had this dream on the eves of Antietam, Gettysburg, and Vicksburg. One such dream encouraged him to move ahead to get the votes for the 13th Amendment. Lincoln considered this one a good word from the Lord. After all, his name means "Lives by the water."

So here he was, a few days into the celebration of General Lee's surrender, and he was having prophetic dreams. His latest of the long series of moving forward in dark waters toward another shore was one he believed to be a sign that Confederate General Joe Johnston would soon surrender to William T. Sherman in North Carolina.

Lincoln's concerns for the perils of reconstruction were actually the work he put in the front of his mind to shake off the foreboding dream of his untimely death.

Speaking from the second-story window, Lincoln addressed a large crowd. Even now, he pushed the envelope of giving freedom to the slaves to another level. Something he had only spoken of privately before, he dared to bring the narrative of Black Americans being able to vote.

"It is unsatisfactory to some that the elective franchise is not given to the colored man." He suggested they start with those who had served in the army. Lincoln wouldn't get the chance to put his Reconstruction policies into effect. That night, one member of the crowd outside the White House was the handsome young actor John Wilkes Booth, who snarled to his companion about Lincoln's address: "That means n— citizenship! Now, by God, I'll put him through. That is the last speech he will ever make."[2]

It was.

And so ended the Civil War with the death of the American president.

RECOGNIZING AND INTERPRETING THE ASSASSINATION AND DEATH OF PRESIDENT LINCOLN

On Good Friday, April 14, 1865, at 10:15 p.m., a shot from a .44 caliber "pocket cannon" rang out in Ford's Theatre. Eight hours later, at 7:22 a.m. on April 15, Doctor Robert King Stone pronounced the 16th president of the United States dead.

"Now he belongs to the ages," Dr. Stone said.

If this was a dream or a prophecy, what would it mean? Could it be interpreted?

Even though all this information is historic and literal fact, it is also filled with prophetic types and symbols for those who have an eye to see and an ear to hear the messages the Lord Almighty has hidden in these well-documented events.

In light of the prophetic dream of our late President Lincoln, what if we looked at his death as if there was a prophetic word in it? What if we could forget for just a moment that this is a true historical event that hit the headlines worldwide? Imagine this was a word from God with prophetic symbolism, type, and shadow. Try to grasp the idea that there is a powerful word from God hidden within the drama of this thunderous event just waiting to be discovered.

Because there is.

THE NUMBERS THAT PROPHESY

To find the gold hidden within this rock, we need to investigate or "search out the matter." Prophetic interpretation of real-time events is the honor and the privilege of God's children.

> *It is the glory of God to conceal a matter, but the glory of kings is to search out a matter* (Proverbs 25:2 NKJV).

As in any dream, if we are going to discover the concealed messages, we would start by noting the symbols and discovering their meanings within the context of the Bible.

Maybe we would start with the meanings of the names of the people involved:

- Abraham: Father of many

- Lincoln: Lives by the water

- Robert: Bright fame or marvelous light

- King Stone: The leader the people rejected (1 Peter 2:4-8)

- Ford: Place to cross a river

As we look with a prophetic eye, we might very well start to see a significant message so obvious that it is begging to be interpreted and brought to light.

We would definitely take note of the day of the event: April 14. April 14 is the 104th day of the year in the Gregorian calendar; 261 days remain until the end of the year.

In interpreting any common dream, we know to look up the Bible verses with 104 connected to them.

The weapons of our warfare are not carnal but mighty in God for pulling down strongholds (2 Corinthians 10:4 NKJV).

Right off the bat, I would know God is saying this is not natural but rather supernatural. God was pulling down the stronghold of slavery in the United States of America and redefining our union. It wasn't only natural warfare—it certainly was spiritual as well.

More significantly, April 14 is also the Feast of Passover. The very day all Jewish people remember the hand of the Lord protecting the firstborn from the angel of death that brought a great judgment to Egypt by pharaoh's own word. This is very important if we believe these are numbers that prophesy.

Again, if just looking at the actual day of the shooting, it's easy to see profound truth in simple facts.

1. Passover is the sacrifice of the lamb. The High Holy Day recognizes the slaves being set free from Egypt. We know Lincoln set the slaves free in America through the passing of the 13th Amendment and winning the Civil War.

2. April 14, 1865, was also Good Friday—the day King Jesus laid down His life at the Cross.

What if you looked up Scriptures with those date numbers—April 14 or 4:14. The well-known Esther 4:14 Scripture surely stands out as Jesus the Lamb and Lincoln the emancipator were in positions: *"...for such a time as this [and for this very purpose]?"* (Esther 4:14 AMP). You go on to discover James 4:14 (NKJV) says that life on earth is merely a "vapor," and John 4:14 (NKJV) promises eternal, "everlasting life."

Lincoln was our country's 16th president. What about the number 16, which represents the love of God? If you know how numbers prophesy, you know the number 16 is where you lay down your life to demonstrate the love of God. Let me show you what I'm talking about.

THE 16TH PRESIDENT AND THE NUMBER THAT PROPHESIES

First Corinthians chapter 13 is known to many as "The Love Chapter." The King James translators tried to come up with another word for the very specific kind of love God shows. They used the word "charity." In our modern language, when we say "charity," we tend to think of soup kitchens and Santa ringing a bell in front of a department store. Understanding this problem, they used the word "charity," meaning the kind of love that comes from God and causes us to give away everything. The love of God is where you lay down your life. That's what the number 16 represents throughout Scripture.

In 1 Corinthians 13, there are 16 attributes to the love of God. Other examples of 16 throughout Scripture include:

- There are 16 "baptisms" throughout the Word.

- There are 16 commands given to the nation of Israel.

- In Acts 15:25, the 16th time Paul's name is mentioned, he is called "beloved."

- There are 16 Jehovah titles in Scripture. This is significant!

- To know God is to love Him, and that is exactly what His Word says.

    Beloved, let us love one another, for love is of God; and everyone who loves is born of God and knows God (1 John 4:7 NKJV).

Though President Lincoln was unable to discern the meaning of his dream about his death, you and I can discover God's Word through the prophetic types and numbers surrounding this historic headline.

And now, as a doctor named Stone declared, "that message belongs to the ages."

PARABLE SUMMARY OF LINCOLN'S ASSASSINATION

The war was over, and the slaves were set free by law, but there was no celebration. Just grief, pain, and a whole lot of anger. An overwhelming sense of loss had moved across both the north and the south. The price we paid as a nation for the outcry of slavery was to see every American cry. The horrors and misery of the Civil War are only rivaled by the horrors and misery of slavery itself.

The population at the time of the war was less than 30 million. By the time the war was over, 624,511 were buried on the battlefield or in Union or Confederate burial sites. If you count that number with those who died of diseases, were shot to pieces, and sent to starve in prison camps, that number nearly doubles to 1,125,453.

This is with a population of less than 30 million! The Civil War affected everyone on the North American continent in a horrible way.

Source: https://commons.wikimedia.org/wiki/File:Lincoln_statue,_Lincoln_Memorial.jpg

Compare this to the horrific effect that Vietnam had on every American. In that war, we lost 58,152 Americans, and this was with a population of more than 200 million. Oh, how it traumatized, polarized, and hurt our country.

It's really unimaginable! One out of 30 people who were alive at the beginning of the Civil War were dead, maimed, or displaced in some way by the end of it. This is not to mention the effect of people who lost their homes, farms, businesses, and even entire cities.

The psyche—soul and spirit—of the United States as a whole and of the people individually was one way before the Civil War, and it was drastically different after the war. For example, in Texas, the male population was wiped out. Only 30 percent of the region where I'm from made it back alive, and the few who did were missing limbs and even their sanity.

Can you imagine 7 out of 10 of all men between the ages of 15 and 50 being killed? An entire generation of kids fatherless and women left to the hardship of raising children on the frontier?

And for what? This is the message of the parable.

As a 6th generation Texan raised by a Texas history enthusiast, I grew up understanding that the Civil War was not fought over slavery. I know that sounds crazy to people raised in any other place at any other time. But we knew it to be true because it was our grandfathers' grandfathers who came back missing something or didn't come back at all.

If you had asked the men from Texas why they were fighting at the time of the war, it was simply because they had to. Duty, family, and the fact that draft dodgers would be killed.

Loyalty to the South was huge. States' rights versus federal rights and the fact that Lincoln wasn't even on the ballot in the election was a big deal to those guys. On top of that, the new Constitutional Union Party led to the formation of the Republican Party in 1856 and the splitting of the Democratic Party in 1860. The Constitutional Union Party was a short-lived vehicle for moderates that collapsed by the start of the Civil War. It succeeded only in helping to disperse the 1860 vote sufficiently to ensure the election of the Republican candidate, Abraham Lincoln.[3] The election of leadership seemed like a sinister circus to the common people of Texas. Washington, DC, was a foreign country to people in the Southwest and a planet away.

There was also the fact that the culture in Texas was one that had just successfully rebelled from Mexico less than 25 years earlier and came from a nation that had successfully rebelled against the British only 70 years before that.

The huge majority of Confederate soldiers fought for the same reason the huge majority of Union soldiers fought. A war started, they were drafted or called, and they simply answered because they were honorable people. When it started, it was not about slavery; it was about loyalty to the Union or loyalty to the South, known as Virginia.

Slavery was the issue of rich people, we thought.

Lincoln didn't think that and neither did the Lord.

Lincoln, moved by the Spirit of God, actually made the Civil War about slavery after the war had already started. He moved the United States into the righteous cause of the emancipation of all negro slaves; and by the grace and hand of God, he succeeded. Most people today don't know history, so they miss the miracle of Lincoln making the war about ending slavery and the unification of our nation.

CIVIL WAR TIMELINE

- The Civil War began Friday, April 12, 1861.

- Lincoln set free all northern slaves, buying each for $300 on April 16, 1862.

- Lincoln's Emancipation Proclamation became effective on January 1, 1863.

- The 13th Amendment was passed by the Senate on April 8, 1864.

- The 13th Amendment by the House of Representatives on January 31, 1865.

- The Civil War ended on April 9, 1865.

- Lincoln was shot on April 14, 1865.

- Lincoln died on April 15, 1865.

- The 13th Amendment was ratified on December 6, 1865 (8 months after the war).

- The 13th Amendment was proclaimed on December 18, 1865.

I have ancestors I'm proud of who fought for Texas. I know their stories and am proud I come from them. Now that I have said that, no matter what the perspective of the common Johnny Reb or Billy Yank of the day, the Civil War was indeed about slavery. God made it about slavery, and it happened on Lincoln's watch and through his leadership.

"The Almighty has His own purposes," Lincoln said in his second inaugural address on March 4, 1865, a mere month before victory.

In his last speech, he didn't brag about his accomplishments or the defeat of the rebels but directed his narrative toward the war's meaning. His conclusion—it was all about ending slavery, and that was in his mind up until a bullet was fired through it.

America paid a terrible price for the atrocity of slavery. The celebration of the war's end was stifled by the mournful wails of all freedom-loving yet grief-stricken people.

The shot that killed President Lincoln sealed a hatred between the North and the South that would carry on to the assignation of President John F. Kennedy a hundred years later.

SUMMARY FACTS

ABRAHAM LINCOLN SUMMARY FACTS

- Abraham Lincoln's name means "Father of many" and "Lives by the water":

  *Seeing that **Abraham shall surely become a great and mighty nation,** and all the nations of the earth shall be blessed in him?* (Genesis 18:18 KJV)

  *That he might sanctify and cleanse it with the **washing of water by the word*** (Ephesians 5:26 KJV).

- Abraham Lincoln was the 16th President of the United States. Sixteen is the number that represents the love of God and when you lay your life down.
- Lincoln was assassinated on Good Friday on the Gregorian calendar and Passover on the Hebrew calendar. Passover is when the blood pays the price of sin through a lamb and Good Friday is the day that Christ, the Lamb of God, paid the price of sin with His blood.
- The date Lincoln died was April 14 (4:14). Read Esther 4:14 and see if you don't think it's a word concerning Abraham Lincoln and the cause of the North:

  For if you remain completely silent at this time, relief and deliverance will arise for the Jews from another place, but you and your father's *house will perish. Yet who knows whether **you have come to the kingdom for such a time as this?*** (Esther 4:14 NKJV)

- The number 14 represents "Generational Promises," where God keeps His Word throughout the generations and answers the prayer of many generations beginning with the original man named Abraham (see Genesis 17:5).

So all the generations from Abraham to David are fourteen generations; and from David until the carrying away into Babylon are fourteen generations; and from the carrying away into Babylon unto Christ are fourteen generations (Matthew 1:17 KJV).

- April 14 is the 104th day of the year: *"The weapons of our warfare are not carnal but mighty in God for pulling down strongholds"* (2 Corinthians 10:4 NKJV).
- Lincoln was shot at 10:15 p.m.: *"As the Father knows Me, even so know I the Father; and I lay down My life for the sheep"* (John 10:15 NKJV).
- Lincoln was pronounced dead at 7:22 a.m. Jeremiah 7:22 (NIV) speaks of the day God set His people free from the slavery of Egypt: *"For when I brought your ancestors out of Egypt and spoke to them, I did not just give them commands about burnt offerings and sacrifices."*
- Lincoln was pronounced dead 9 hours and 7 minutes after he was shot. Isaiah 9:7 is the well-known Messianic promise that Jesus would show up to redeem His people and bring judgment and justice through His Kingdom.

Of the increase of His government and peace there will be no end, upon the throne of David and over His kingdom, to order it and establish it with judgment and justice from that time forward, even forever. The zeal of the Lord of hosts will perform this (Isaiah 9:7 NKJV).

The Civil War was indeed about God's interference into our nation's slavery atrocity. With it, He brought judgment and justice. Never in the history of the world has God torn apart and divided a nation for the sake of the slaves within it. Especially a nation that began with a covenant with God.

But these slaves were different. These slaves cried out to the Lord God Jehovah in the name of Jesus. They whispered illegal prayers at the iron kettles they turned over and knelt down to pray before these makeshift altars. They identified as God's children and sang praises of hope in Christ as they toiled in relentless chains. They sang of God's goodness in the face of humankind's worst evil.

God heard their cry. He heard their whispers. He heard their groans of the heart; and all those who refused to hear their cries in their day, wept with a great thirst that was not quenched in their lifetimes.

There was no celebration on behalf of the North or the South at the end of this war. Just a reminder that it takes one to lay down his life to set the slaves free. A prophetic word pointed not to a man in 1865 named Abraham but to the original Abraham some 4,000 years earlier. The father of our faith.

And what about the covenant our great nation had with God? What about the prayers of all those people who suffered so greatly calling Jesus Lord, leaving homelands behind to settle in a land of freedom? When they landed in the "New World" in 1620, sadly slavery had already been introduced by seafaring explorers and pirates.

Many will say to Me in that day, "Lord, Lord, have we not prophesied in Your name, cast out demons in Your name, and done many wonders in Your name?" (Matthew 7:22 NKJV)

You know the rest of it, and did you catch the Scripture number? It matches the exact time of Lincoln's death (7:22 a.m.). These are numbers that prophesy. Each person, whether they can hear it or not, is responsible for heeding this powerful message.

NOTES

1 Ward Hill Lamon, *Recollections of Abraham Lincoln 1847-1865* (Lincoln, NE: University of Nebraska Press, 1994), 116-117.

2 Sarah Pruitt, "What Lincoln Said in His Final Speech," *History.com,* October 18, 2023; https://www.history.com/news/what-lincoln -said-in-his-final-speech; accessed December 12, 2023.

3 "Constitutional Union Party," *Britannica;* https://www.britannica .com/topic/Constitutional-Union-Party; accessed December 12, 2023.

"Mathematics is the language with which God has written the universe."
—Galileo Galilei, Astronomer, Physicist, Engineer

"History is the unrolled scroll of prophecy."
—James Garfield, 20th US President

"If you don't know history, then you don't know anything. You are a leaf that doesn't know it is part of a tree."
—Michael Crichton, Prolific Writer, Filmmaker

2

PROPHETIC HISTORIC EVENT 2

THE RMS TITANIC

Source: Sinking of the Titanic. (2024, September 26). In Wikipedia. https://en
.wikipedia.org/wiki/Sinking_of_the_Titanic

Since the first prophetic event focused on the death of President
Abraham Lincoln, it is only fitting that the second prophecy in the
headlines would be the Titanic. Why? The dates are exactly the same.
President Lincoln was shot on April 14 and died on April 15. Similarly, the Titanic hit an iceberg on April 14 and sank on April 15. The
difference is 47 years.

Dates, timing, and the numbers do matter to the Lord. This is not a coincidence. It's a prophetic marker.

You may know that 47 is the atomic number for silver. Silver is symbolic of redemption. But the kicker in this case is that Isaiah 47 is all about the fall of Babylon!

Just like President Lincoln's death was prophesied days earlier through a dream, the sinking of the Titanic was prophesied by two famous writers years before the event.

Prophetic Message

The Prophetic Word in the Sensational Headlines: "The Fall of Babylon"

W.T. Stead was the inventor of modern tabloid media. Widely hailed as the greatest newspaperman of his age, he invented investigative journalism, making the reporter's experience a big part of the story. This guy was something else.

One of the things I appreciate about him is that he fought the sexualization of kids. Through him, the age of consent in Britain was actually raised from 13 to 16 years old through "The Stead Act." Why was it named after him?

Stead actually bought a 13-year-old girl, proving it was easy to traffic children by documenting the purchase and reporting that it was legal to abuse her because of lax national law. In 1885, doing such a thing became a criminal offense in Britain, carrying a sentence of 3 months.

Stead's crusade against child prostitution made for sensational headlines and interesting reading; he published a series of four articles titled, "The Maiden Tribute of Modern Babylon."

Source: https://commons.wikimedia.org/w/index.php?curid=70567661

In this chapter, you will learn that Stead is not only the father of shocking headlines but also actually died on the maiden voyage of the Titanic. The Titanic represents the Babylon spirit all of us have to "jump ship."

His documented tabloid did a lot of good and sold a lot of newspapers, but it didn't bring him closer to the Lord. Stead was the son of a pastor and knew his Bible well. But his desire to investigate, experience, and document taboo and edgy content led him into dark places. He became interested in all kinds of spiritualism away from the throne of King Jesus.

Leaving his heritage, Stead became interested in speaking to the dead. As this progressed into an obsession, he consulted witches and held demonic seances. He invited something he called "automatic writing," where he would become demonically possessed and write crazy things he shouldn't have been able to know.

"I have learned I will either be hanged or I will drown," Stead reported from his future. The direct fate had not been determined or revealed by his deceased informer. Despite the dire report, he continued to investigate and report the more edgy topics of British society.

He even used his dramatic flair to write and print a fictional story titled, "How the Mail Steamer Went Down in Mid-Atlantic, by a Survivor." In it, Stead tells the prophetic story of an unnamed ocean liner that tragically sinks in the Atlantic. In his fictional tale, the good guy grows concerned over a noticeable lifeboat shortage on deck. Nobody listens, and as it goes, the liner hits a small ship in the fog. As the ocean liner sinks, women and children are given priority on the lifeboats, but chaos takes over, and only 200 passengers and crew members of the original 700 people on board survive the disaster.

"This is exactly what might take place and what will take place if the liners are sent to sea short of boats," he declared in his story. Astoundingly, this same man lost his life on the maiden voyage of the RMS Titanic 26 years later because it was short of lifeboats.

A NIGHT TO REMEMBER FROM THE FUTURE

Stead boarded the Titanic for a visit to the United States to take part in a peace congress at Carnegie Hall at the request of President William Taft. Survivors of the Titanic reported he told wild stories about a cursed mummy in the British Museum through the 11-course meal that fateful night.

According to a writing by Joseph O. Baylen, after the ship struck the iceberg, Stead helped several women and children into the lifeboats. Then, in an act "typical of his generosity, courage, and humanity," he gave his life jacket to another passenger.

According to Reverend Curry Blake, Stead had offered popular missionary and faith healer John G. Lake a first-class ticket on the Titanic's first and last trip. Lake turned him down.

A POINTER TO THE PROPHETIC?

Let's review the facts:

- Stead is known as the father of investigative journalism, tabloid newspapers, and modern sensationalistic headlines.

- Writes and prints his most impactful work titled, "The Maiden Tribute of Modern Babylon."

Source: Morgan Robertson. (2024, September 26). In Wikipedia. https://en.wikipedia.org/wiki/Morgan_Robertson

- Declares he will die from hanging or drowning.

- Writes and prints a fictitious work about a steam liner that sinks in the Atlantic and the tragic results of not having enough lifeboats.

- Declares this is exactly what will happen if ocean liners do not increase the number of lifeboats on board.

- Dies on the Titanic's maiden voyage because there were not enough lifeboats.

Another Prophetic Declaration in Print Before the Headline

Fourteen years before the Titanic disaster, *The Wreck of the Titan: Or, Futility* was a short book written by Morgan Robertson and published as *Futility*.

It features a fictional British ocean liner named Titan that sinks in the North Atlantic after striking an iceberg on a cold April night.

The story's main focus is a Titan naval officer who finds God, gets the love of his life back, and fights alcoholism after the Titan's sinking. Comparisons between the historic record of the Titanic and Robertson's fictional work about the Titan are nothing short of remarkable.

Both were the world's largest steamships. Both were called unsinkable and "the greatest works of mankind." Both the real Titanic and the fictional Titan collided with an iceberg on an April night and only had the minimal number of lifeboats the law required.

Though God does not cause these tragedies, He employs them to speak to each generation. How and what does it mean? Why would there be prophetic pointers in print before the headlines actually happened? They were used to establish the fact that there was a prophetic word in the event of the Titanic.

...By the mouth of two or three witnesses every word shall be established (2 Corinthians 13:1 NKJV).

THE GLORIOUS TITANIC

The Titanic was the biggest, most luxurious, fastest, and most incredible moveable object that mankind had ever built.

Back in 1912, not even homes had electric heat and lights, but this amazing vessel had four 400-watt generators that ensured every room on board was lit up like noonday. She had every modern convenience known to man. There was incredible artwork, including carvings and paintings. The interior was filled with luxurious couches, unbelievable architecture, and crystal chandeliers. The silver forks and spoons were the finest in the world and everything had the White Star company name stamped on it.

There was more than $11 million worth of wine on board and five grand pianos. The Titanic was the first ship with a gymnasium, the first with a swimming pool, and the first ship with a barber shop and hair salon.

The Titanic was one of the very first ships equipped with the brand-new technology of a wireless telegraph system. People in first class could send postcards by Morse Code from the middle of the Atlantic. The Italian inventor, Guglielmo Marconi, who invented this wireless telegraph and won the 1909 Nobel Prize in Physics, was offered free passage on the Titanic but had taken the Lusitania 3 days earlier.

The world had never seen anything like the Titanic on land or at sea. She was a moving example of excellence in every way. A first-class ticket on that maiden voyage cost the equivalent of $130,000 today.

If you had the money and were able to go, wouldn't you have jumped at the opportunity? I know I would have. However, there were a few famous people who were supposed to be on board but didn't make it for one reason or another. These people became notorious for missing the boat.

THE JUST-MISSED-IT CLUB

In addition to John G. Lake and Guglielmo Marconi, Robert Bacon, the United States ambassador to France, just missed it. Others who missed traveling on the Titanic's maiden voyage include Milton Hershey, the chocolate maker; Edward Selwyn, the man who built the Selwyn Theatre on Broadway; Alfred Vanderbilt from the famous Vanderbilt family; and even JP Morgan himself had a ticket. Fortunately, they joined the just-missed-it club.

God did a miracle of protection for the Reverend James M. Gray. He missed the boat as did the Reverend Stuart Holden.

John Mott, an influential evangelist and longtime YMCA official who shared the Nobel Peace Prize in 1946, is also in the club. He and a colleague were offered free passage on the Titanic by a White Star Line official interested in their work, but they declined. Instead, Mott and his colleague took the humbler liner, Lapland. According to a biography by C. Howard Hopkins, when they reached New York and heard about the disaster, "It is said that the two men looked at each other and agreed: 'The Good Lord must have more work for us to do.'"

I would like to think that we would all be part of the "Just-Missed-It Club" and avoid a Titanic disaster. I think the prophetic message shows us how.

THOUGHT TO BE "JUDGMENT-PROOF"

The ship was captained by Edward J. Smith, known as "The Millionaire Captain." Smith gave the command to leave the harbor and steam toward New York. On the day Titanic left South Hampton, people stood all along the coasts to get a glimpse of "the proudest accomplishment of man the world had ever seen."

Any kind of disaster or even mishap was unthinkable on her maiden voyage and the proverb of the day was that "God Himself could not sink it!" But history proves the Titanic was not unsinkable. The Titanic was unsavable, however, and there is a message for all of us in the why.

ADVANCING THE JUDGMENT AND BECOMING A BYWORD

Now, what I am about to tell you is about prophetic "type." God did not cause this event to happen. He caused His voice to be upon it.

> *The voice of the Lord is over the waters; the God of glory thunders; the Lord is over many waters* (Psalm 29:3 NKJV).

Psalm 29 says the voice of the Lord is upon the waters, and this is especially true when it comes to the prophetic parable of the Titanic. This disaster didn't happen to these people because they were bad. This was a tragic event designed by hell and partnered with humankind. God causes all things, even bad things, to work together for good for those who love Him and are called according to His purpose (Romans 8:28 NKJV).

So, let's look at the prophetic parable of the Titanic and turn to see the voice as John did in Revelation chapter 1.

And I am very sore displeased with the heathen that are at ease for I was but a little displeased, and they helped forward the affliction (Zechariah 1:15 KJV).

"Forward the affliction" literally means to advance judgment or bring on disaster. The Titanic is a case in point, or a perfect prophetic example, of how to advance judgment and bring on a disaster in your life. This ship should be known for her beauty and her accomplishments. She was a dream and a vision that was actually fulfilled by thousands of people working hard to bring it to fruition.

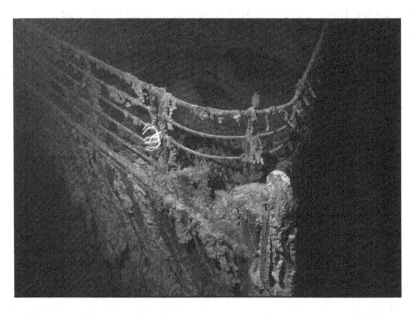

Source: https://commons.wikimedia.org/wiki/File:Titanic_wreck_bow.jpg

But she's not.

The Titanic is a byword—a proverb in our generation for disaster and failure. It is a slogan or a catch phrase for something big and doomed. When you see something that has become a byword on a worldwide scale, that is God speaking. The Lord said in Deuteronomy that your actions can cause your judgment to be known among all peoples.

> *And you shall become an astonishment, a **proverb**, and a **byword** among all nations where the Lord will drive you* (Deuteronomy 28:37 NKJV).

The word *astonishment* means a thing of horror. When God brings an advanced disastrous judgment, He makes His enemy like this:

> *...a **byword** among the nations, a shaking of the head among the peoples* (Psalm 44:14 NKJV).

In other words, people will look at you the way they look at a bloody car wreck. This thing of horror will become a modern-day slogan or a byword that represents something terrible that people will talk about and shudder.

This is what the Titanic looks like today.

More than 12,600 feet down and crushed under 2.4 miles of ocean, she lays in ruin as a byword, and people can't look at her enough.

> *The more they increased, the more they sinned against Me; [therefore], I will change their glory into shame* (Hosea 4:7 NKJV).

What took more than 3,000 workers 3 years to build took 2 hours and 40 minutes to sink and about 8 minutes to go from the surface to the ocean floor.

Sadly, 1,517 is the number of people who died in the frigid 28-degree water.

According to the American Red Cross, a water temperature of 79 degrees can lead to death after prolonged exposure, while 50 degrees can cause death in an hour, and 32 degrees can be lethal in 15 minutes.

Many of the 713 survivors reported the sound of more than 1,300 people swimming in the frigid water after Titanic sank—the rest were trapped beneath in the lower decks. The simultaneous yelling for help sounded like "the crowd at a football or baseball game." Others reported those in the waters looking for a lifeboat went into a long continuous chant before going "deathly silent" after about 20 minutes.

Their pleas for help fell upon what we proverbially call "deaf ears" as those in the lifeboats sat silently in the dark for fear their own boats would be turned over.

Just like the headline written by Robertson 14 years earlier, that's an overarching prophetic theme in this event—the "Futility" of crying for help when you ignore the warnings from the Lord.

TWO MAJOR PROPHETIC WARNINGS

The maiden voyage of the Titanic was an international event on the waters between continents, so I believe this to be a word for all nations and all people.

The first step those involved took to bring disaster upon themselves and advance God's judgment is that they did not glorify

God. They only sought glory for themselves, their name, and their accomplishment.

1. WHEN GOD IS NOT GLORIFIED, DISASTER FOLLOWS.

> *So the last shall be first, and the first last. For many are called, but few chosen* (Matthew 20:16 NKJV).

The first of her voyages was the last of her voyages. Titanic is the picture of what happens when you glorify yourself. Remember, on the day that Titanic left South Hampton, it was said people stood all along the coasts "to get a glimpse of the proudest accomplishment of man the world had ever seen."

Not only did they not glorify God, they rubbed their own glory in God's face, believing there were no consequences for doing so. It was actually said that "God Himself could not sink this ship," or so they thought.

> *As they were increased, so they sinned against me: therefore will I change their glory into shame* (Hosea 4:7 KJV).

> *...so that they are without excuse: because that, when they knew God, they glorified him not as God, neither were thankful; but became vain in their imaginations, and their foolish heart was darkened. Professing themselves to be wise, they became fools* (Romans 1:20-22 KJV).

> [The whore of Babylon] *Reward her even as she rewarded you, and double unto her double according to her works: in the cup*

which she hath filled fill to her double. How much she hath glorified herself, and lived deliciously... (Revelation 18:6-7 KJV).

The Titanic is a prophetic symbol of a people, a nation, a generation, or even a church that is so big, modern, cutting-edge, and luxurious, it boasts of its own glory—and downgrades, even ignores or refuses, God's glory.

The primary purpose why God created us is to give Him glory. How awesome we are, should prove how awesome God is. If our glory only boasts of how big and grand we are, no matter what we advertise, we will soon find out we are not unsinkable. Each of us, as pictured in the Titanic, has fallen short of the glory of God, and our humility to God is paramount.

The prophetic picture here is that when something boasts of its own beauty and power against God, He will cause those things to become a slogan, or byword, of the exact opposite. He will give it a completely different branding strategy and one we will not like.

In the case of the Titanic, the byword is straight out of Mark 9:35 (NKJV) where Jesus says, *"If anyone desires to be first, he shall be last of all and servant of all."* The first voyage of Titanic was indeed her last because she was *"titanic,"* and not small in her own sight.

The voice of God is described as "still" and "small" in 1 Kings 19:12. The year 1912 is exactly when this event took place. What is the prophetic word here?

If we are too big and too busy, we will miss His voice altogether and run straight into a monstrous disaster.

The second major prophetic warning:

2. WE MEET DISASTER WHEN WE DON'T HEED THE WARNING TO STOP AND CHANGE COURSE.

On April 14, 1912, the Titanic radio room crew received several messages warning them of the danger ahead. There is a prophetic message in the names of the ships that tried to get the Titanic to change course:

- The *Corona,* which means "crown"

- The Dutch liner *Nordom,* meaning "expert explorer"

- The *Baltic,* which means "white water" or "belt"

A German liner, the Amerika, sent a message warning of a monster iceberg that would be hard to see in the moonless night. Amerika means "home ruler."

At 7:30 p.m., another 3 messages from the USS Californian were intercepted, warning of ice only 50 miles ahead. California means "hot furnace" or "mythical land." Because they kept the furnace hot as they sped across the Atlantic in great haste to break the time set by the White Star line's sister ship, the Olympic, the Titanic became literal mythos for generations to come. Then, at 9:40 p.m., they received another warning from the SS Mesaba. Mesaba is a Hebrew word that means *"turn around."*

The millionaire captain didn't heed the warnings because he thought he was the exception to the rule. It could happen to everybody else, but it wouldn't happen to him. He was commanding the Titanic.

The radio men halted the warnings being received because the transmissions interfered with their ability to send postcards from the first-class passengers to their friends and family on land. These transmissions would become haunting reminders of Vanity Fair before impending demise.

Men by the name of Bride and Phillips were in charge of the radio room. They ignored all warnings because they were too concerned with sending the messages from their rich and famous passengers. In their minds, the Titanic was too big for it to hit anything and the radio room was too busy to heed the red flags being sent to it.

This misplaced reasoning advances the picture of judgment from Zechariah 1:15.

At 10:55 p.m., just some 10 to 20 miles away, the Californian sent the most critical warning. Commanded by Captain Stanley *Lord,* the California warned it was stopped in ice. Lord sent a warning, and Officer Bride received it. Again, frustrated at the interference of the incoming message as he was trying to send a stack of "Wish you were here" telegraphs, Bride rebuked the Californian with this infamous reply and insult:

"KEEP OUT. SHUT UP. YOU'RE JAMMING MY SIGNAL!"

When the *Bride* of Christ, which is the church, turns to the *LORD* Jesus and says, "Keep out. Shut up. You're jamming my signal," there's a monster mountain out there with her name written all over it—an unavoidable disaster.

> *Because they did not obey the voice of the Lord their God, but transgressed His covenant...and they would neither hear nor do them* (2 Kings 18:12 NKJV).

Hear, O earth! Behold, I will certainly bring calamity on this people—the fruit of their thoughts, because they have not heeded My words nor My law, but rejected it (Jeremiah 6:19 NKJV).

...to be a curse, and an astonishment, and an hissing, and a reproach, among all the nations whither I have driven them: Because they have not hearkened to my words, saith the Lord, which I sent unto them... (Jeremiah 29:18-19 KJV).

Unable to save the Titanic, Captain Lord shuts down his radios, turns off the lights, and orders his crew to go to sleep until sunrise.

SOMETHING IN THE DARK— UNIMAGINABLE AND INVISIBLE

There was no moon that night and not a ripple on the sea. The only light was coming from the Titanic itself, which made it very difficult for the lookout men to see past the bow of that lit-up ship. A party was in full swing. The professional music from the world-famous orchestra and the laughter of guests must have bounced off the still water and amplified back to the enjoyment of the men on watch.

Gradually, the yellow glow from the liner began to light up a literal mountain of ice looming in the dark directly in front of them. The iceberg was much higher than the top deck of the ship. I can't imagine how terrifying it must have been to finally see that the deck had been stacked against the Titanic all along.

It was an unthinkable ship-killer. A rare lunar event occurring brought the highest tides in 1,400 years. It dislodged millions of tons of ice from the shallow waters of Newfoundland, sending it all south into the shipping lanes.[1]

The odds of such a thing were literally astronomical. The moon being at its closest proximity to Earth in 14 centuries in tandem with the closest approach to the sun for the entire year guaranteed a fixed glacier could actually be free floating.

Because the moon had not risen and there were no winds at all to splash on this glacial killer, it was invisible until there were only 37 seconds to impact. Even though it was directly in front of them.

Had they hit it dead-on, it is believed the boat would never have sunk. However, in trying to avoid it, the monster mass of ice gouged a rip through 6 of the "air-tight" compartments. Had they not passed by it, it is possible they could have used the frigid mountain itself to shelter people while they waited for rescue.

So, the collision only caused a thud while the Titanic, at full steam ahead, continued into the dark. Most were convinced it was a near-miss, and many didn't even realize anything major had happened.

THE PARTY CONTINUES

Amazingly, when the Titanic hit the iceberg, a bunch of snow fell off onto the main deck. Again, try to imagine how huge this iceberg must have been. People came outside, picked up the snow, and had a snowball fight, never realizing they were on a doomed ship heading straight for their ultimate judgment. They couldn't see the rip in the hull beneath the water. They were bleeding to death and had no idea that one way or another, they would soon be in the 28-degree ocean water, in the pitch dark, with almost 13,000 feet of water below them.

Bride had already assured that nobody was coming to help them. The men working the radio room understood what the passengers did not and quickly changed their insults to SOS signals.

A DEAF EAR WILL GET YOU A DEAF EAR

Immediately, Bride and Phillips began to reach out to all those who had been reaching out to them just hours earlier.

The *Californian* was just a few miles away. Some say as few as 10 ships were nearby; others say as many as 16. The *Titanic's* Captain Smith ordered bright-colored flares to be sent up to signal for aid. At first, passengers came out with their martinis to awe at the festive rockets. They were soon ordered to put on life jackets, and the narrative began to change. The party was abruptly over.

But the *Californian's* Captain Lord did not hear their cries nor see their bright signals for help in the otherwise completely dark night. He had turned off his radio and turned in to bed after Bride's insulting rebuke.

> *...for I will not hear them in the time that they cry unto me for their trouble* (Jeremiah 11:14 KJV).

Bride kept banging his finger on the telegraph hoping to be interrupted by an incoming response: "We're sinking fast. Cannot last much longer. Need help immediately."

Proverbially, even prophetically, his transmissions fell on deaf ears.

YOU ARE ON YOUR OWN

Captain Smith went to his crew in that last hour and declared, "You've done your duty. It's every man for himself now."

Though this may seem noble, it is also prophetically terrifying. In the hour when you hit that unavoidable mountain in your path, the devil you trusted—who told you to ignore all the warnings—will abandon you to the coming terror. The very one you trusted to lead you will thank you for your service and leave you to face the dark, cold water by yourself.

When Judas went to the religious leaders of his day and asked for help because he had sold out an innocent Man, Jesus, they told him in essence the same thing, "You are on your own."

> *Saying, "I have sinned by betraying innocent blood." And they said, "What is that to us? You see to it!"* (Matthew 27:4 NKJV)

In other words, "You deal with it." Ultimate doom is hard to imagine when things look great and are working right. It is also difficult to visualize the terror that comes with this kind of disaster. If you won't glorify God and won't heed His warnings, you're going to find the disaster God was talking about is far worse than you ever imagined, and you have nobody to blame but yourself for the horrifying outcome.

THE COMFORT ZONE

Do you remember what I told you about Zechariah 1:15, where God says He is sorely displeased at the heathen who were at ease? Why did the Lord bring that up? Because He can't deal with people who value their comfort more than anything else.

When the word got out that the ship was sinking, the crew didn't even fill the lifeboats to capacity because they didn't want to put the first-class guests in any kind of discomfort. Hundreds more could have been saved had they not placed their comfort first. Comfort is an ultimately selfish agenda, and selfishness reeks in the nostrils of God, who is anything but self-centered.

It's All Over but the Shouting

A man named Thayer recorded that the anguish in the cries of the people suffering the frigid water "became a *long continuous wailing chant.*" The imagery of wailing and gnashing of teeth is exactly the prophetic picture of the darkness Jesus describes as the fate of those who have rejected the voice of the King:

> *Then the king said to the attendants, "Bind him hand and foot, take him away, and cast him into outer darkness; there will be weeping and gnashing of teeth"* (Matthew 22:13 NKJV).

Summary of the Prophetic Parable of the Titanic

The RMS Titanic was the largest, most luxurious, technologically advanced cruise ship in White Star's line. The Bible calls Jesus Christ "the bright and morning star." While this achievement was meant to bring glory to God, it instead was used to glorify the strength and brilliance of humans.

It was prophesied in print 28 years prior to the actual event by W.T. Stead, the father of sensational headlines, tabloid journalism, and investigative journalism. He was famous for writing "The Maiden Tribute of Modern Babylon" and "How the Mail Steamer Went Down in Mid Atlantic, which did not have enough lifeboats." He died on the maiden voyage of the RHS Titanic, which was woefully short of lifeboats.

The sinking of the world's most glorious cruise ship was prophesied in print 14 years before the actual event in a short book originally titled *The Wreck of the Titan: Or, Futility*. Written by Morgan Robertson, it was published under the title *Futility* in 1898. In this work of fiction, the name of the ship that struck an iceberg and sank in the Atlantic on a cold April night was "The Titan."

...By the mouth of two or three witnesses every word shall be established (2 Corinthians 13:1 NKJV).

The assassination of President Lincoln and the tragedy of the sinking of the Titanic are connected through the same dates. President Lincoln was shot on April 14 and died on April 15. The Titanic struck the iceberg on April 14 and sank 2 hours and 40 minutes (a total of 160 minutes) later on April 15.

This event took place in 1912. In 1 Kings 19:12, the voice of God is described as still and small. The Titanic was too big, and the radio room was too busy to hear the still, small voice of God.

When God is not glorified, you invite disaster. The first of her voyages was the last of her voyages. The Titanic is a picture of what happens when you glorify yourself.

The practical reason the ship sank is because those who were trusted with decisions over the trip didn't heed the warnings to change their course.

On April 14, they received multiple warnings from 6 different ships:

- The Corona meaning "crown"

- The Nordom meaning "expert explorer"

- The Baltic meaning "white dangerous water"

- The Amerika meaning "home ruler"

- The Mesaba meaning "turn around"

- The Californian meaning "hot furnace"

From a prophetic perspective, these names could be translated into something like this: Your King (Corona), the One who goes before you (Nordom), warns you of dangerous water ahead (Baltic). I'm the boss (Amerika). So, turn around (Mesaba) or face judgment (Californian) in the hell you are bringing upon yourselves.

The last and most important warning comes from the Californian commanded by Captain Stanley Lord, who was stopped in the ice. Captain Lord sent a warning, and Officer Bride received it in the Titanic radio room. Bride's rebuke and insult was, "Shut up. Keep out. You're jamming my signal." When the *Bride* of Christ, which is the church, turns to the *LORD* Jesus and says, "Keep out. Shut up. You're jamming my signal," it is not unsinkable. It is actually unsavable.

Captain Lord turned off his radio at the insulting rebuke of Bride and never heard the Titanic's cries for help.

The people went into the water where there was wailing and gnashing of teeth in the very frigid water. The Titanic sank to the bottom of the sea, and 1,517 people died.

The 1517th verse in the Bible is Genesis 50:10 NKJV: *"...and they mourned there with a great and very solemn lamentation...."*

The more they increased, the more they sinned against Me; I will change their glory into shame (Hosea 4:7 NKJV).

And so it is with the historical event of the sinking of the RMS Titanic. A word for all of us today.

THE NUMBERS THAT PROPHESY

Now that the stage is set with facts in the historical account and prophetic pictures in the names connected to the ominous sinking of this stellar feat of mankind, let's take a look at the "hidden" meanings of the numbers within the story to see what God is speaking through this headline.

It was 47 years from the day that Lincoln was shot when the Titanic hit the iceberg and 47 years to the day that Lincoln died when the Titanic sank.

The number 47 on the atomic scale is the number for silver, which means a work of the Redeemer. In this case, it speaks of judgment. Isaiah 47 is the prophetic promise of the fall of Babylon.

The Fall and Humiliation of Babylon

Isaiah 47 (NKJV)

1

"Come down and sit in the dust,
O virgin daughter of Babylon;
Sit on the ground without a throne,
O daughter of the Chaldeans!
For you shall no more be called
Tender and delicate.

2

Take the millstones and grind meal.
Remove your veil,
Take off the skirt,
Uncover the thigh,
Pass through the rivers.

3

Your nakedness shall be uncovered,
Yes, your shame will be seen;
I will take vengeance,
And I will not arbitrate with a man."

4

As for our Redeemer, the Lord of hosts is His name,
The Holy One of Israel.

5

"Sit in silence, and go into darkness,
O daughter of the Chaldeans;
For you shall no longer be called
The Lady of Kingdoms.

6

I was angry with My people;
I have profaned My inheritance,

And given them into your hand.
You showed them no mercy;
On the elderly you laid your yoke very heavily.

7

And you said, 'I shall be a lady forever,'
So that you did not take these things to heart,
Nor remember the latter end of them.

8

"Therefore hear this now, you who are given to pleasures,
Who dwell securely,
Who say in your heart, 'I am, and there is no one else besides me;
I shall not sit as a widow,
Nor shall I know the loss of children';

9

But these two things shall come to you
In a moment, in one day:
The loss of children, and widowhood.
They shall come upon you in their fullness
Because of the multitude of your sorceries,
For the great abundance of your enchantments.

10

"For you have trusted in your wickedness;
You have said, 'No one sees me';
Your wisdom and your knowledge have warped you;
And you have said in your heart,
'I am, and there is no one else besides me.'

11

Therefore evil shall come upon you;
You shall not know from where it arises.
And trouble shall fall upon you;
You will not be able to put it off.
And desolation shall come upon you suddenly,
Which you shall not know.

12

"Stand now with your enchantments
And the multitude of your sorceries,
In which you have labored from your youth—
Perhaps you will be able to profit,
Perhaps you will prevail.

13

You are wearied in the multitude of your counsels;
Let now the astrologers, the stargazers,
And the monthly prognosticators
Stand up and save you
From what shall come upon you.

14

Behold, they shall be as stubble,
The fire shall burn them;
They shall not deliver themselves
From the power of the flame;
It shall not be a coal to be warmed by,
Nor a fire to sit before!

15

Thus shall they be to you
With whom you have labored,
Your merchants from your youth;
They shall wander each one to his quarter.
No one shall save you."

Let's look at some specific numbers:

6 – Flesh of man

There were 6 ships that warned the Titanic. In the supernatural, this number has to do with man's opposition to God and man's pitiful stance against God. It is the number God uses to preach about how we fall short and how messed up we are. Six is what happens when you add your works (6) to His grace (5) and when you fall short of His perfect Spirit (7).

It also speaks plainly of humanity, either in concert with God or in opposition to God. We will have much more to study about this in the next chapter on Neil Armstrong's landing and the prophetic man on the moon.

Draw your own conclusions, but the pattern of man and 6 is amazingly powerful throughout God's Word. It was also a literal red flag of warning from the 6 ships trying desperately to warn the Titanic and save the 2,200 souls aboard. When you choose the flesh of man and pride of life over the glory of God, you've doomed yourself.

14 – Generational Promises, Fear of the Lord, His Witness

Remember, the written prophetic works that spoke prophetically of this by Stead and Robertson were 14 years apart. The last one was 14 years before the sinking of the Titanic.

Fourteen is the number that points to, or stands as a witness to, the Spirit of God (7 x 2) moving and made manifest. It has to do with God's Spirit perfecting something and the drastic measures He will take to make things right, including saying, "I warned you of this happening." Just as the makers of the Titanic and those connected to its demise had a choice—glorify God or themselves—the number 14 has both positive and negative meanings throughout the Word of God.

The name "David" has a gematria, or numeric value, of 14, as do the words "hand" and "gold." This prophetically shouts that when we seek God's hand in our lives, His glory (gold) will fall on us and our endeavors. In the New Testament, the verbs "to bear" and "shepherd" are used 14 times each. Jesus bore our sins and was glad to "shepherd" us as His sheep.

Also in the positive, it was on the 14th day of the month, Nisan, when God Almighty kept His promise of over 400 years to bring Israel out of slavery in Egypt (Exodus 12:6-36). Thus, 14 signifies generational promises kept. Check out this in-your-face example of 14 as generational promises:

> *So all the generations from Abraham to David are **fourteen generations**, from David until the captivity in Babylon are **fourteen generations**, and from the captivity in Babylon until the Christ are **fourteen generations*** (Matthew 1:17 NKJV).

I can't help but think about the 14 ascending and 14 descending days of the moon in terms of God's promises to the church, His bride. She has no light but reflects the light of the sun. The Lord is referred to as the "sun" in two key Scriptures that each have a message for the Titanic:

> *For the **Lord God is a sun** and shield; the Lord will give grace and glory; no good thing will He withhold from those who walk uprightly* (Psalm 84:11 NKJV).

The choice was theirs. God wanted to bless the Titanic, but the people in charge chose cursing instead through their pride and arrogance. Remember the meaning of the name "Californian" and those burning hot coals in the engine room as the doomed ocean liner streaked across the Atlantic at full speed?

> (The Great Day of God) *"For behold, the day is coming,* **burning like an oven,** *and all the* **proud,** *yes, all who do wickedly will be stubble. And the day which is coming shall burn them up," says the Lord of hosts, "That will leave them neither root nor branch. But to you who fear My name* **The Sun of Righteousness** *shall arise with healing in His wings; and you shall go out and grow fat like stall-fed calves"* (Malachi 4:1-2 NKJV).

Just like that, Catholics observe 14 "stations of the Cross," which depict the suffering of Jesus. In the Bible's prophetic book, titled Proverbs or prophetic parables, the expression *"fear of the Lord"* occurs 14 times in the King James Version. Proverbs 8:13 says the fear of the Lord is to love what God loves and hate what He hates. God hates pride. So should we.

15 (date Titanic sank) – Rest, Overcoming Death, Perfect Grace (3x5), also represents a time of consecration

The number 3 represents "perfect completion," while 5 represents "grace" throughout the Bible. Grace is the God-given ability to overcome something bad. With 15, we have grace perfectly completed where we enter into God's rest—a place where we are not continually striving but walking in grace and blessing.

Three times each year, Israel rested on the 15th day of the month (Leviticus 23:6-7; 23:34-35; Esther 9:20-22). I believe 15 is prophetically associated with special times of being consecrated to the Lord.

That means we rule and reign by the power of God, the way God rested (or celebrated) over His creation after He had finished His works.

By God's grace, we ultimately overcome even death itself. When we die, we rest. So when you see the number 15, you tend to see the grace to overcome death, or rest, as you might say. Examples of 15 as perfectly completed grace to overcome death or rest include when Noah was on the ark. The waters rose to 15 cubits above the highest mountain before the ark rested on the mountains of Ararat. Noah and his family survived what killed the rest of the world.

According to Esther chapter 9, the Jews overcame those trying to exterminate them on the 15th day of the month of Adar. They overcame a death sentence from their enemies. In 2 Kings chapter 20, Hezekiah was granted 15 additional years of life. He overcame a timeline that most others don't. Finally, it is recorded that Bethany, where Jesus raised Lazarus from the dead, is 15 furlongs from Jerusalem.

4/14 (date) – Strong's Concordance #414 anektoteros, meaning more tolerable.

Through this number, as well as the number 14, God is preaching fear of the Lord and being a witness of Him and His majesty. Those aboard saw their generational promises stripped from them as they sank to their deaths in the frigid waters of the North Atlantic. There are 6 verses in Scripture that use the Greek word *anektoteros* as translated "more tolerable" (Matthew 10:15; 11:22,24; Mark 6:11; Luke 10:12,14) and all are connected to judgment for not welcoming the people of God and refusing to have fear, or respect, for His name. None says it better than Mark chapter 6 (flesh of man) verse 11 (judgment over disorder).

*And whoever will not receive you nor hear you, when you depart from there, shake off the dust under your feet as a testimony against them. Assuredly, I say to you, it will be **more tolerable** for Sodom and Gomorrah in the day of judgment than for that city!* (Mark 6:11 NKJV)

4/15 (date) – Strong's Concordance #415 aneleemon, meaning without compassion, cruel, lacking mercy.

This word is found in one verse in the Bible, and it's a doozey! It's the list of 23 (death) things that result from God respecting our wishes and giving us over to the hell we so desperately want to partner with. These all end one place—judgment.

And since they did not see fit to acknowledge God or consider Him worth knowing [as their Creator], God gave them over to a depraved mind, to do things which are improper and repulsive, until they were filled (permeated, saturated) with every kind of unrighteousness, wickedness, greed, evil; full of envy, murder, strife, deceit, malice and mean-spiritedness. They are gossips [spreading rumors], slanderers, haters of God, insolent, arrogant, boastful, inventors [of new forms] of evil, disobedient and disrespectful to parents, without understanding, untrustworthy, unloving, unmerciful [without pity] (Romans 1:28-31 AMP).

The most Googled 4:15 verse in the Bible is in the book of Ephesians. It speaks of those righteous captains who tried to warn the Titanic but warned in vain. To do anything else would have been cruel and lacking in mercy.

Instead, speaking the truth in love, we will grow to become in every respect the mature body of him who is the head, that is, Christ (Ephesians 4:15 NIV).

The book of Mark talks about good, life-saving words falling to the ground—or, in the case of the Titanic, falling on "deaf ears" of those with too much to do and too much pride to listen. Since the calamity took place over two dates, I include both for you to consider:

The sower sows the word. And these are the ones by the wayside, where the word is sown. When they hear, satan comes immediately and takes away the word that was sown in their hearts (Mark 4:14-15 NKJV).

As long as we are looking at the span of the dates, let's look at verses 414 and 415 in the Old Testament. They very well may testify to the Titanic account.

Then Abraham fell on his face and laughed and said in his heart, "Shall a child be born to a man who is one hundred years old? And shall Sarah, who is ninety years old, bear a child?" And Abraham said to God, "Oh, that Ishmael might live before You!" (Genesis 17:17-18 NKJV)

What?! God gives a generational promise to a childless geriatric, and Abraham chooses something lesser—something he has created by his own will and rebellion. Ishmael was not the son of the covenant, yet Abraham was asking God to bless and glorify what God did not create. Talk about ripped from the prophetic headlines! Now let's look in the New Testament for verses 414 and 415 written in Jesus's day. Wait for it...

> *"He who has ears to hear, let him hear!" And the disciples came, and said to Him, "Why do You speak to them in parables?"* (Matthew 13:9-10 NKJV)

My friend, you can't make this stuff up! Not only did radio operator Bride not have ears to hear, our friend W.T. Stead, though an investigative journalist, totally missed the prophetic parable he was living out as he boarded what he had prophetically titled "The Maiden Tribute of Modern Babylon" to his own demise.

1912 (year) – Strong's Concordance #1912 epibareó, meaning to put a burden on.

Looking at the three occurrences of this word, all in the New Testament, it's a word on humility—not wanting to be a burden; rather, putting others first and not taking advantage by wanting something for free, but paying the price.

> *But if anyone has caused grief, he has not grieved me, but all of you to some extent—not to **be too severe*** (2 Corinthians 2:5 NKJV).

> *For you remember, brethren, our labor and toil; for laboring night and day, that we might not **be a burden** to any of you, we preached to you the gospel of God* (1 Thessalonians 2:9 NKJV).

*Nor did we eat anyone's bread free of charge, but worked with labor and toil night and day, that we might not **be a burden** to any of you* (2 Thessalonians 3:8 NKJV).

Many aboard the Titanic paid the price—the ultimate price—for the lack of humility among the ship's leadership. The decisions of a handful of men brought judgment on many, leaving few with a way of escape.

(Sodom and Gomorrah Destroyed) *Then the men said to Lot, "Have you anyone else here? Son-in-law, your sons, your daughters, and whomever you have in the city—take them out of this place!* (Genesis 19:12 NKJV)

28 (water temperature) – Times and Seasons.

Twenty-eight is the number associated with the beginning and the end of certain God-given timelines. Ecclesiastes chapter 3 lists 28 times and seasons for every purpose under Heaven. Check out the following words on time and timelines from the Bible associated with the number 28:

- Twenty-eight times the word "weeks" appears as a measure of time.

- The phrase "day and night" appears exactly 28 times throughout Scripture.

- There are 28 days in a lunar month. The Hebrew calendar is a lunar calendar.

- Calendar years normally follow a 28-year cycle. Since there are 7 days in a week and leap year occurs every 4 years, a calendar from 28 years ago is the same as the one you're looking at.

- Twenty-eight is definitely connected to the calendar. In fact, 28 is the number of days in the shortest month of the Gregorian calendar. February has 28 days, except in leap years when there are 29 days. All 12 months of the Gregorian calendar have at least 28 days, regardless of the year.

The word *cross* shows up exactly 28 times in the Bible, noting the ultimate sacrifice of laying down his life for another. There are 28 crosses—one for every time and every season in your life. Similarly, the phrase "end of the world" is found 28 times throughout Scripture. A definite picture of a timeline, "end of the world" doesn't just mean the end of the humanity on planet Earth. Loosely translated in modern terms, it could also mean the "end of your rope." We've all been there and most aboard the Titanic were literally at the end of their rope as well as the end of their timeline.

12,600 feet (official depth of where Titanic sits)

Nevertheless, death reigned from Adam to Moses... (Romans 5:14 NKJV).

From the fall of Adam to the death of Moses, if you add all their life spans together, it equals exactly 12,600 years![2]

The value of 12,600 is a variant of 1,260, known from prophecies about the apocalypse, or "unveiling" of Jesus, only multiplied by 10. This prophetic number of 1,260 days equals three-and-a-half years or 42 months (Revelation 11:2-11; 12:4-6,11; 13:5). This is when God

1	Adam	930	10	Noah	950	19	Terah	205
2	Seth	912	11	Shem	600	20	Abraham	175
3	Enosh	905	12	Arpachshad	438	21	Isaac	180
4	Kenon	910	13	Shelah	433	22	Jacob	147
5	Mehalalel	895	14	Eber	464	23	Levi	137
6	Jared	962	15	Peleg	239	24	Kohath	133
7	Enoch	365	16	Reu	239	25	Amram	137
8	Methuselah	969	17	Serug	230	26	Moses	120
9	Lamech	777	18	Nahor	148		**Total 12,600**	

judges and brings great tribulation to where sin wants to rule and reign.

1517 (approximate and official number who perished)

Do you remember the name of Robertson's prophetic fictional work? It was *The Wreck of the Titan*. It was later released under the single-word title *Futility*.

> *And if Christ is not risen, your faith is futile; you are still in your sins!* (1 Corinthians 15:17 NKJV)

Robertson nailed the ship's name and how and when it would sink. I think he even prophetically dialed in on the official number of deaths on board because this verse speaks of what Paul called "futile faith" set apart from the resurrection of King Jesus. Of course, it would come as a severe warning.

1517 – Strong's Concordance eirénopoieó, meaning to make peace.

And that's exactly what each person on that ship was forced to do— make peace with their Maker whether they knew King Jesus or not.

When I think about how afraid these people must have been and how helpless they must have felt in the face of such a hopeless situation, I have to remind myself that God is good and He was there with each one of them. Every. Single. Soul. That includes you reading this today.

And by Him to reconcile all things to Himself, by Him, whether things on earth or things in heaven, having made peace through the blood of His cross (Colossians 1:20 NKJV).

The choice is yours just as it was theirs in their great day of distress. Verse 1517 in the New Testament prophesies of those who raise their fist and refuse to choose Jesus.

And Peter, remembering, said to Him, "Rabbi, look! The fig tree which You cursed has withered away" (Mark 11:21 NKJV).

2200 (approximate number of souls on board) – Double meaning Strong's Concordance zestos means boiling hot, and zeiq means to cry, call.

There is a big argument on the exact number of those who perished on the Titanic. Some fact sites say 2,222, some 2,223, and others 2,229. So I'm going to say 2,200-plus, as nobody truly knows. You will find something very interesting when you look up the number 2200 in Strong's Concordance. Not only was the engine room "boiling hot" and speeding these unknowing people to their doom, but the vast majority of them cried out—desperately called for help—and found none in the glacial waters.

And when he came to the den, he cried out with a lamenting voice to Daniel. The king spoke, saying to Daniel, "Daniel, servant of the living God, has your God, whom you serve continually, been able to deliver you from the lions?" (Daniel 6:20 NKJV)

Do you think God wanted to save the Titanic? He did! He placed 6 ships within proximity to offer help. He sent warning after warning through those ships. They could have been delivered, but those making the decisions that fated night told their Deliverer to not only keep out but shut up. That's not how the bride should treat her Lord. He desires a passionate bride whose heart is on fire for His agenda and His plan of salvation.

*I know your works, that you are neither cold nor **hot**. I could wish you were cold or **hot**. So then, because you are lukewarm, and neither cold nor **hot**, I will vomit you out of My mouth* (Revelation 3:15-16 NKJV).

"Hot" here is the Greek word *zestos* mentioned previously. Just like the more than 2,200 souls aboard the Titanic, no one knows the hour or the day of our last breath of Earth's air. No matter the day, God Almighty is looking for people whose hearts are burning for Him. The alternative is unthinkable, just as the ship was thought to be unsinkable. Don't be unsavable! Run after Jesus and make Him your Lord and Savior today. This brings me to our final subject where the Titanic is concerned—the "Just-Missed-It Club."

As you read about earlier, there are 12 famous members of an elite group called the "Just-Missed-It-Club." They could actually be confirmed as having bought tickets for the maiden voyage yet were not on board for one reason or another. Of course, there is a prophetic word being spoken through this as well.

Looking at the numbers that preach, **12** represents God's perfect government throughout Scripture. Twelve is the last of the 4 numbers God uses to show His perfection. It's also the number that shows He is in control and actively ruling as King. When the Lord wants to show us there is a perfect plan, He likes to use the number 12 in His language.

Think about it. Jacob had 12 sons. Israel had 12 tribes. Jesus had 12 disciples. He set up the church with the foundation of 12 teachable, yieldable men who would drop their plans and follow Him anywhere. That's why the New Jerusalem has 12 gates and 12 foundations. After Peter defended Jesus by cutting off Malchus's ear in the Garden of Gethsemane in Matthew 26:53 (NKJV), Jesus told Peter to put away the sword because *"Do you think that I cannot now pray to My Father, and He will provide Me with more than twelve legions of angels?"*

There are also 12 pearls and 12 angels associated with the New Jerusalem. The measurements of that city are listed as 12,000 furlongs, or stadia, while the wall will be 144 (12 x 12) cubits (Revelation 21:16-17). Speaking of Revelation, the famous 144,000 (12 x 12) are redeemed from the 12 tribes of Israel in chapter 14.

So why all the information about the number 12 as God's perfect government? Because this number literally shouts, "I have a plan. It is perfect and I have a purpose for it and each one of them." Who are they? Let's find out.

Source: J. P. Morgan. (2024, September 26). In Wikipedia. https://en.wikipedia.org/wiki/J._P._Morgan

JOHN PIERPONT MORGAN

JP Morgan formed United States Steel, the world's first billion-dollar corporation. Created General Electric. Saved the US banking system during the Panic of 1907, earning the title "The Napoleon of Wall Street."

Because of his high interest in the White Star Company that owned the Titanic, he was, for all intents and purposes, the owner of the ship.

He was on vacation in France for his health. At the last minute, decided to prolong his vacation and missed the Titanic's maiden voyage.

Source: https://commons.wikimedia.org/wiki/File:Assistant_Secretary_of_State
_Robert_Bacon.jpg

ROBERT BACON

Robert Bacon was the US Ambassador to France. Worked with JP Morgan in forming US Steel and the International Mercantile Marine Company. His replacement as ambassador was late to arrive, causing a delay. He had to stay in France to help Myron T. Herrick transition into the position and missed his passage on the Titanic to his new career at Harvard University. Bacon later sailed home on the SS France's maiden voyage from La Havre (safe haven, place of safety and rest) with his family, April 20, 1912.

Source: https://commons.wikimedia.org/wiki/File:Milton_S._Hershey,_1910.jpg

MILTON HERSHEY

Milton Hershey started Hershey Chocolate Company. His chocolate factory, built in Pennsylvania, resulted in a town growing up around it named after Hershey. He and his wife financed good works and many public facilities there.

Hershey and wife, Catherine, were vacationing in France because of Catherine's poor health. The warm climate in Nice was thought to help.

Needing to attend to business, Hershey left three days early on the *Amerika*, instead of using his tickets for the Titanic. The Amerika was one of the ships that sent warnings to the Titanic.

Source: https://commons.wikimedia.org/wiki/File:John_Raleigh_Mott.jpg

JOHN R. MOTT

John R. Mott was a dedicated Christian. National Secretary for YMCA. Later part of Student Volunteer Movement for Foreign Missions. Traveled the globe teaching on Christian values; crossed the Pacific Ocean 14 times and the Atlantic Ocean 100 times.

The White Star Line offered him and a companion free passage on the maiden voyage. They were uncomfortable traveling on such a luxurious ship and declined the generous offer. They traveled on the *Lapland* instead. When they heard of the tragedy of the Titanic, they looked at each other and said, "The Good Lord must have more work for us to do." Mott shares a Nobel Peace Prize with Emily Balch for establishing Protestant Christian organizations.

Source: https://commons.wikimedia.org/wiki/File:Guglielmo_Marconi.jpg

GUGLIELMO MARCONI

Guglielmo Marconi was the inventor of wireless telegraphy. Awarded 1909 Nobel Prize for Physics. Was offered free passage on the Titanic by White Star while vacationing in England. He had to get to NYC earlier than expected and needed a ship with a stenographer to take dictation during the passage. He left on the Lusitania three days before the maiden voyage of the Titanic.

His family was to follow on Titanic but his son became sick, causing his wife to delay their departure. Marconi was investigated because it was thought that his wireless operators withheld information on Titanic to sell to newspapers. Both Marconi and the operators were cleared when it was proven that his operators aboard the Titanic had saved more than 700 people.

REVEREND J. STUART HOLDEN

Reverend Holden was a Christian speaker. Vicar of St. Paul's Church in London. He booked first-class passage on the Titanic because he was invited to speak at the Christian Conservation Congress at Carnegie Hall on April 20, 1912.

His wife fell ill, so he decided to take care of her and miss the maiden voyage of Titanic. When he heard of the Titanic tragedy, he mounted his ticket to a frame with the words of Psalm 103, "Who Redeemeth Thy Life From Destruction" in gratitude. Other clergymen who were expected at the conference and set to sail on Titanic were Archbishop Thomas J. Madden and Reverend J.S. Wardell Stafford. They were also prevented from taking the maiden voyage of Titanic for various reasons. Holden's ticket is the only known surviving first-class ticket from the Titanic. In 2003, it was put on display at the Liverpool Merseyside Maritime Museum.

DAVID BLAIR

Blair was the Titanic's Second Officer during her sea trials and journey from Belfast to Southampton. He was later moved to Titanic's sister ship, the Olympic. The transfer happened so hastily that he accidentally left the Titanic's crow's nest binoculars in his cabin without telling anyone where they were. He also mistakenly took the key to the crow's nest telephone.

EDGAR SELWYN

Edgar Selwyn was founder of Metro Goldwyn Mayer (MGM).

He attempted suicide at age 27 by jumping into the Chicago River. He landed on ice and lived. In April 1912, Selwyn delayed his trip home on the Titanic to finish a novel, *The Reagent*.

Source: https://commons.wikimedia.org/wiki/File:EdgarSelwyn_
AmericanStage_NYPL.jpeg

When he returned to America, he experienced the greatest success of his career with two musicals: "The Wall Street Girl" and "Within the Law." Instead of dying, he earned a million dollars from "Within the Law" just before the roll-out of federal income tax in 1912. Yes, the Titanic sunk on what will forever be known as "Tax Day" in the United States.

ALFRED, TOM, AND BERTRAM SLADE – THE SLADE BROTHERS – FIREFIGHTERS

The 3 brothers were all experienced sailors and signed on as firemen on the Titanic April 6, 1912. At 8 a.m. on April 10, just after reporting aboard Titanic, the brothers and other crew went to one of Southampton's pubs. Having to wait for a long train, the brothers were late returning. They made it to the White Star dock at 11:59 a.m., just as the gangplank was being drawn up. The officer in charge refused to lower it and allow them to board. He'd already replaced them with other sailors desperate for work. The Slade brothers' replacements did not survive. However, the other two sailors who went to the pub with them and made it back in time to board Titanic did survive. They were John Podesta and William Nutbean.

JOSEPH DONON – CHEF

Donon was 24 years old. Henry Clay Frick, an associate of JP Morgan, tipped Donon 20 gold dollar pieces and offered him a job as his personal chef in the US. Both the Fricks and Donon were booked for Titanic's maiden voyage, but Mrs. Frick sprained her ankle delaying their trip for two days.

Donon left America to fight for France in World War I. He returned after the war and became the personal chef to Mrs. Hamilton Twombly, daughter of William H. Vanderbilt. After all, George Vanderbilt had tickets on the Titanic for himself and his wife, Edith, in early 1912. "We have it in writing," notes Lauren Henry. "It's not a legend. It's a fact that Mr. and Mrs. Vanderbilt were booked to be on Titanic."

THOMAS HART – FIREFIGHTER

On May 1912, *The New York Times* headline was *"Thought to be lost–Alive,"* referring to Thomas Hart. He was thought to have drowned. Thomas Hart was an actual ship firefighter but through false information and media frenzy, was assumed to have been on the Titanic. It is also surmised Thomas Hart had his identity stolen by James Hart (pictured) who was actually signed up to the Titanic and did not survive.

For the remainder of his life, Thomas Hart was introduced as having survived the Titanic. Thomas never even signed up for the maiden voyage and lived his life explaining that he had not drown in the ice cold waters of the Atlantic.

SUMMARY FACTS

LESSONS LEARNED FROM THE TITANIC AND THE NUMBERS THAT PROPHESY

While it was a miracle of sorts to be among the 713 survivors in a life-boat, it was best not to go aboard this cursed ship to begin with. You can avoid being on a disastrous path like this by simply doing this:

- Do not be too big (Titanic) or too busy with your own agenda (the radio room operators) and refuse to hear the still, small voice cited in 1 Kings 19:12. The timing of this event was 1912 and, in your own timeline, be prepared to quickly stop and pivot when God gives His warning. Radio operator Bride rebuked Captain Stanley Lord, and I remind you that we are the bride of Christ, and Jesus is our Lord. The word "Lord" is in the Bible 6,781 times. Yahweh, Jehovah, and Adonai are the Hebrew words typically translated as "Lord," which means "land owner." Jesus is the Ruler who owns everything. More than that, it means He owns the responsibilities of His covenant because He loves us and knows us personally. He wants to save us, not just from disasters in the natural, but from eternal death in hell.

- Humble yourself. Stop your busyness. Hear His still, small voice and make sure you are savable. Join the real "Just-Missed-It Club" by crying out to King Jesus and asking Him to save you and yours before you experience further disaster.

NOTES

1 Jayme Blaschke, "The Iceberg's Accomplice: Did the Moon Sink the Titanic?" *University News Service,* March 5, 2012. Astronomers from Texas State University-San Marcos stated, "...the lunar connection may explain how an unusually large number of icebergs got into the path of the Titanic." https://news.txst.edu/about/news-archive/press -releases/2012/March-2012/Titanic030512.html; accessed December 13, 2023.

2 Jeremy Northcote, "The lifespans of the patriarchs: Schematic orderings in the chrono-genealogy," *Vetus Testamentum* (2007), 243-257, especially pages 245, 247.

"Symbols are the language of something invisible spoken in the visible world."
—Gertrud von Le Fort

"History is a vision of God's creation on the move."
—Arnold J. Toynbee

"Science has not yet mastered prophecy. We predict too much for the next year and yet far too little for the next 10."
—Neil Armstrong

Prophetic Historic Event 3

"Man" on the Moon

Source: https://www.nasa.gov/image-detail/337294main-pg62-as11-40-5903-full

This chapter is a prophetic word for all humankind in achieving the ultimate and overcoming fear, sin and death—the dramatic headlines of the Apollo 11 moon landing and the "man" on the moon.

Prophetic Message

On July 18, 1969, Bill Safire typed a speech for President Nixon titled, "In event of moon disaster." This would be the White House's response should the unthinkable happen, and they were thinking about it a lot. Portions of the speech:

> Fate has ordained that the men who went to the moon to explore in peace will stay on the moon to rest in peace. These brave men, Neil Armstrong, and Edwin Aldrin, know that there is no hope for recovery, but they also know there is hope for mankind in their sacrifice....

> ...For every human being who looks up at the moon in the nights to come, will know that there is some corner of another world that is forever mankind.

By the hand of God on the strong arm of an astro-pilot with a prophetic name, President Nixon didn't have to deliver this sad speech. But two days later, as Apollo 11's lunar module "Eagle" plummeted toward the moon's surface, it looked like a crash was inevitable.

On July 20, around 9 minutes before touchdown, Armstrong realized they were going to overshoot their landing site. Alarms were sounding, and the lunar surface was getting closer and closer. He estimated by sight and his mathematical genius that they would overshoot by approximately 3 miles. His guess was close, and they actually missed by 4.

Armstrong quickly modified his flight plan and set a course to try and land somewhere without boulders and craters. Aldrin, Armstrong, and "a bunch of guys turning blue" in Houston had to find another suitable place to safely touch down in a matter of seconds.

Program alarms were screaming, radio communications with Mission Control were patchy and distorted, and they were burning more fuel than calculated.

Passing what Flight Controller Steve Bales called "The deadman's curve," they descended past the altitude of being able to abort the landing. It was going to happen now, right or wrong.

Long before the computer age, these men were using math based on Newtonian physics and measured with stopwatches. They were writing with grease pencils and calling out numbers.

According to his stopwatch, Bob Carlton, measured less than 30 seconds of fuel from his Houston desk as Armstrong guided the Eagle softly down onto its impromptu landing site. But just before landing, as he watched from his tiny window, Neil Armstrong saw a huge crater where they were supposed to land and boulders everywhere. He had to cross over them before touching the surface. Then, 12 seconds later, the pods touched dust, and they quickly shut down the engine.

Bob looked at his stopwatch marked with scotch tape—18 seconds of fuel remaining in the tank.

The Eagle had landed, and that previously unmapped few feet of the moon became "Tranquility Base"—the first human outpost on the moon.

"Houston, Tranquility Base here. The Eagle has landed."

Charlie Duke responded. "Roger, Twan—Tranquility, we copy you on the ground. You got a bunch of guys about to turn blue. We're breathing again. Thanks a lot."

The world celebrated.

The date in 1969 was July 20 or 7/20.

Wherefore by their fruits ye shall know them (Matthew 7:20 KJV).

The Numbers That Prophesy

One Small Misstep in a Giant Footnote of History

Six hours later, Armstrong stepped out, and for a 20-minute period before Buzz Aldrin stepped out of the Eagle, Neil Armstrong was the man on the moon.

His name is prophetic and so are his first words with his first step. Armstrong stepped off Eagle's footpad and declared, "That's one small step for man, one giant leap for mankind."

Source: https://www.nasa.gov/image-detail/amf-as11-40-5877

Armstrong intended to say, "That's one small step for a man," but he later admitted that he accidentally left the "a" out of his well-rehearsed first words. He got a little tongue-tied and messed up his amazing quote, but I believe it was the Lord who caused it to happen.

Once it was spoken, it couldn't be undone, which brings me to this next chapter in *Numbers That Prophesy*.

The 6th word Armstrong spoke on the moon was "man," and his first sentence ended with mankind. It was a mistake for the man, but it was prophetic from God.

When the 6th word is the word "man," you can see a prophetic marker that points us to the 6th book of the New Testament—and the only book in the Bible with the word "man" in its title, Romans.

In fact, not only the man on the moon but the man in the New Testament likes to say "man" as the 6th word. "Man" is the 6th word in a total of 6 verses in Romans. Remarkable! (See King James/New King James versions of Romans 2:1,3,6; 3:28; 5:7; 6:6).

If you're not sure of the mathematical miracle, look at this. "Man" is the 6th word in Romans 6:6, which speaks volumes in light of this story we are studying:

Knowing this, that our old man is crucified with him [Jesus], *that the body of sin might be destroyed, that henceforth we should not serve sin* (Romans 6:6 KJV).

Let's count them—11 words from the guy from Apollo 11, and "man" was the 6th word spoken to mankind from the moon.

1   2   3   4   5   6   7   8   9   10   11

"That's one small step for man, one giant leap for mankind."

Before we get into the number 11, let's stay on track with the 6 of mankind.

THE SIX OF MANKIND

In order to see the prophetic fingerprint of the Lord and hear His amazing message through those thunderous headlines, we have to really understand God's language through the number 6. The number for human beings, mankind and the flesh of man is the number 6. Redeemed or not, He stamps the number 6 on it.

Maybe somebody noticed this when they saw the Apollo spacecraft—command module and lunar module—were flying to the Moon at 24,000 miles per hour. That's 6 miles every second.

Maybe they started to see a prophetic pattern when they noticed the moon was 240,000 miles away. That's 6 x 40,000.

Perhaps somebody caught it when President Nixon made the greatest long-distance phone call in all history to speak to them. You can't get a signal today but somehow the 37th president's big-knuckled finger dialed 666666 and spoke to them live in front of the world.

Maybe somebody raised an eyebrow when they saw that the recovery vehicle was Helicopter 66 of the US Hornet.

I think the point of the 6th word from the man on the moon is to see Romans 6:6 and answer the flesh with the cross of Christ. A worldwide word for all mankind.

> *Knowing this, that our old man is crucified with Him, that the body of sin might be done away with, that we should no longer be slaves to sin* (Romans 6:6 NKJV).

Source: https://www.nasa.gov/image-detail/amf-as11-40-5880

SIX IS A NUMBER THAT PROPHESIES

In the natural, the number 6 has an amazing pattern, throughout history and in the Scriptures, as being God's watermark for an authentic production of the flesh. We know the flesh is in opposition to the Spirit. Public enemy #1 is not the devil or the world. The biggest problem anyone has to deal with is the very flesh they are wrapped in and that grayish, wrinkled, 6 pounds of flesh between their two ears.

The following are some examples in Scripture of 6 as the number for "man."

- Man was created on the 6th day.

- Six days of work ordered to man.

- The 6th character in the Bible is the serpent who deceived man and took his authority and place on earth.

- There are 6 words in Hebrew that we translate into the English word "serpent."

- God flooded the whole world when Noah was 600 years old (Genesis 7:6,11).

- There was a giant who had 6 fingers on each hand and 6 toes on each foot (2 Samuel 21:20).

- Goliath's height was 6 cubits and a span (1 Samuel 17:4).

- The 6th commandment of the Ten Commandments is, *"You shall not murder"* (Deuteronomy 5:17).

- The descendants of Cain only go to the 6th generation.

- Evil Queen Athaliah's reign was 6 years (2 Kings 11:3; 2 Chronicles 22:12).

- Six earthquakes in the Bible.

- Six drunks in the Bible.

- Six examples of sorcery or divination in the New Testament.

- Six times Jesus was accused of having a devil.

- Six times Jesus was told to prove Himself with signs and miracles.

- All 6 of the letters that represent the number system of the Roman Empire added together yield the number 666: I = 1; V = 5; X = 10; L = 50; C = 100; D = 500.

> *Here is wisdom. Let him who has understanding calculate the number of the beast, for it is the number of a man: His number is 666* (Revelation 13:18 NKJV).

Now when God is doing a work in mankind, the redeemed side of the 6 coin looks like this biblically:

- Abraham interceded on behalf of the people of Sodom 6 times (Genesis 18:16-33).

- Leah had 6 sons (Genesis 30:19-20; 35:23).

- The Israelites were to gather manna for 6 days (Exodus 16:5,22,29).

- The glory of the Lord covered Mount Sinai for 6 days on behalf of mankind (Exodus 24:16).

- The gold lampstand in the Tabernacle (which signified Jesus being the Light to mankind) had 6 branches coming out of it (Exodus 25:32-35; 37:17-21).

- Two onyx stones, each with 6 names of the sons of Israel were put on the ephod of the High Priest (Exodus 28:9-12).

- There were 6 "cities of refuge" in the land of the Levites (Numbers 35:6,13,15).

- After 6 days, Jesus took Peter, James, and John up the mountain for the Transfiguration (Matthew 17:1; Mark 9:2).

- In the 6th month of Elizabeth's pregnancy, the angel Gabriel appeared to Mary to announce she would give birth to Jesus (Luke 1:26,36).

- In Jesus's first miracle, He changed 6 water pots into wine (John 2:6-10).

- Mary anointed Jesus's feet 6 days before Passover (John 12:1-3).

- At about the 6th hour, Pilate said to the Jews, *"Behold your King"* (John 19:14).

- The world turned dark beginning at the 6th hour Hebrew time (noon) when Christ was on the Cross (Matthew 27:45; Mark 15:33; Luke 23:44).

- In Roman time the 6th hour is 6-7 a.m. when Jesus was being tried by the Roman governor Pilate (John 19:14).

- Jesus suffered on the Cross for 6 hours (He suffered that man may be saved); from 9 a.m. (see Mark 15:25) the hour of the first daily sacrifice in the temple to 3 p.m., (see Mark 15:33-34; Matthew 27:45; Luke 23:44) the hour of the last sacrifice.

- When Peter received his vision from God opening the door to the Gentiles, it was the 6th hour (Acts 10:9).

- There are 66 books in the Bible. God's Word given to mankind.

So when God created man on the 6th day, He stamped the number 6 on him physically. Six especially speaks of the physical body. Check this out:

- There are 6 major members in the human body: head, torso, 2 arms, and 2 legs.

- The average body contains approximately 6 quarts of blood.

- In the average body, the blood travels 12,000 miles (2,000 x 6) in one day.

- The average human heart, beats 72 (12 x 6) times a minute.

- There are 60,000 (6 x 10,000) miles of blood vessels in the human body.

- The average lung weighs about 600 grams.

- The average lung capacity is 6 liters.

- There are 600 muscles in the human body.

- There are 6 primary systems in the human body: skeletal, circulatory, muscular, nervous, digestive, and reproductive.

- The standard measure height for a man is 6 feet.

- The average weight at birth is 6 pounds.

- We like to bury our dead 6 feet down.

Crazy isn't it? The number that prophetically speaks of mankind is the number 6.

MOON DUST AND THE MAN FROM DUST

After subsequent missions to the moon, all 12 men who walked on the moon, performed their tasks, gathered their rocks, and climbed back on board for a long ride home all agreed that the moon smelled like gunpowder. No astronaut walking on the moon's surface has ever removed their helmet and taken a whiff. Instead, the smell of the moon lingers in the dust on their suit and on the rocks brought back to the ship.[1]

The smell, though, got the Apollo 11 crew's attention because there had been a seriously considered theory that moon dust might ignite upon pressurization when oxygen hit it. Imagine the inside of Eagle blowing up or catching on fire while astronaut Michael Collins looked down from 66 miles above the surface of the moon from the command module.

Another huge concern was that the dust would be thick on the moon and act like quicksand when they landed. They really didn't

Source: https://www.nasa.gov/image-detail/as11-40-5875large

know until they landed, but by the grace of God, the theory proved wrong.

The 3 astronauts were actually quarantined after returning because of the supposed threat of dangerous pathogens lying dormant in the dust that could kill all of us on Earth. (Like the Covid mask mandates that would plague the world 53 years later, it was really just theater to show some form of responsible precaution.)

For 21 days, those first-to-the-moon astronauts had to look at the world through a thick piece of glass, and they didn't like it.

"Look at it this way," [Collins] added. "Suppose there were germs on the moon. There are germs on the moon, we come back, the command module is full of lunar germs. The command module lands in the Pacific Ocean, and what do they do? Open the hatch. You got to open the hatch! All the damn germs come out!"[2]

Out of all the dangers of getting to the moon and back, moon dust is considered one of the greatest problems. It destroys the lungs and is toxic to humans. It destroys equipment and fabrics. Ground-up lunar rock, known as regolith, clogs drills, and other delicate instruments, and it's so sharp that it scratches space suits. Because the dust absorbs sunlight, it can also overheat sensitive electronics.

Dust is mentioned 102 times throughout Scripture. (The same number of pilgrims who made the 66-day journey on the Mayflower.) The first time is found in Genesis 2:7 (KJV):

And the Lord God formed man of the dust of the ground, and breathed into his nostrils the breath of life; and man became a living soul.

Did you notice that man is the 6th word in the first verse about dust? There it is again!

So there is no way to escape the biblical and Kingdom connection to the dust of the earth and man, nor the dust of the moon and man.

A Prophetic Look at Astronauts as Type and Symbol

Neil Armstrong

Armstrong was an Eagle Scout who got his pilot's license before his driving license. How prophetic is that?

Source: https://www.nasa.gov/image-detail/amf-9018112

Neil was born on August 5, 1930, in Wapakoneta, Ohio. He was an Air Force test pilot and NASA inventor with an IQ of 139.

There aren't any photographs of Neil on the moon. His footprint is the most famous photograph on the planet and you can see his reflection in his famous photo of Buzz, but there isn't a clear photo of him.

BUZZ ALDRIN

Aldrin's mother's maiden name was Moon. No kidding. How prophetic is that?!

Buzz Aldrin was born on January 20, 1930, in Montclair, New Jersey. His parents—Marion Moon and Edwin Eugene Aldrin—named him Edwin. Edwin got his nickname from his little sister, who couldn't say "brother," so she called him "buzzer." His parents shortened the name to "Buzz." In 1988, Aldrin officially and permanently changed his name to Buzz.

Source: https://www.nasa.gov/image-detail/amf-s69-31743

Aldrin holds three patents and the Guinness World Records lists him as the oldest person to have visited the North and South Poles. Since I mentioned the Titanic in this book, you might want to know that Buzz has actually seen it in person. In 1996, he went to the depths in a tiny sub and viewed the wreckage in person.

Buzz took Communion on the moon. On July 19, 1969, Aldrin and Armstrong had to wait several hours before they could leave the spacecraft, so Buzz used the time to take Communion.

As an elder at Webster Presbyterian Church in Texas, Aldrin had received permission to bring bread and wine into space. After taking Communion, he later said, "...In the one-sixth gravity of the moon, the wine curled slowly and gracefully up the side of the cup." In Aldrin's 2010 memoir, he wrote, "We had come to space in the name of all mankind—be they Christians, Jews, Muslims, animists, agnostics, or atheists. But at the time, I could think of no better way to acknowledge the Apollo 11 experience than by giving thanks to God."[3] He would later call it "A Thanksgiving for all mankind."

Michael Collins

Born on Halloween in Rome, Italy, Michael was the son of a US Army Major General. After becoming a West Point graduate, he eventually became a Major General himself.

I think it's interesting that Collins was actually most famous for what he didn't do—he never walked on the moon. He flew 240,000 miles to the moon on Apollo 11 but never set foot on it. He was also known as "the loneliest man in human history" by TV anchors. All by himself in the Command Module Columbia, 66 miles above the far side of the moon for any amount of time is a long period of time.

Source: https://www.nasa.gov/image-detail/amf-s69-31742

He wasn't lonely, though. He was aware of his isolation and later wrote in his book *Carrying the Fire,* "I feel this powerfully—not as fear or loneliness—but as awareness, anticipation, satisfaction, confidence, almost exultation. I like the feeling."

What the world mistook as lonely, Micheal Collins experienced as exclusive.

While he orbited the moon alone in the command module, Michael Collins knew that he'd live in notoriety if Neil Armstrong and Buzz Aldrin didn't survive the trip. That wouldn't be good. He also knew he wouldn't be remembered if they succeeded, and he was fine with that. He did not want to come home alone. He wrote a note while his two fellow travelers were walking on the moon:

> My secret terror for the last 6 months has been leaving them
> on the moon and returning to Earth alone; now, I am within
> minutes of finding out the truth of the matter. If they fail to
> rise from the surface, or crash back into it, I am not going to
> commit suicide; I am coming home, forthwith, but I will be
> a marked man for life and I know it.[4]

Collins is also known for having "missed the moment." As Neil Armstrong was exiting the lander, Collins's orbit took his command module behind the far side of the moon, cutting off his radio communications. So he never heard the famous line by Armstrong as almost a billion other people did live. By the time he was back in touch, Armstrong and Buzz Aldrin were already planting an American flag on the moon's surface, with the world watching.

Such selfless service and faithful commitment.

Summary Facts

Prophetic Summary of the Apollo 11 Crew

- Armstrong means "strength"

- Aldrin means "old, wise king" or "song of glory"

- Collins means "victory"

> *The Lord is my strength and my song; he has given me victory.*
> *This is my God, and I will praise him—my father's God, and I*
> *will exalt him!* (Exodus 15:2 NLT)

This verse actually has all 3 names in the first part! *"The Lord is my strength* (Armstrong) *and my song* (Aldrin); *he has given me victory"* (Collins).

Source: https://www.nasa.gov/image-detail/
american-flag-heralds-flight-of-apollo-11-2/

Now, if you can bear it, the numbers in Scripture actually match the numbers of the moon landing.

According to the July 20, 2019, *Forbes* article, "Apollo 11's 50th Anniversary: The Facts and Figures Behind the $152 Billion Moon Landing," the exact number of the cost is the number of the Scripture that carries all 3 names—$152 billion and Exodus 15:2.

Do you know why? Because the Author of the Bible and the One who made it happen are both the same person.

Source: https://www.nasa.gov/image-article/apollo-11-official-crew-portrait

THE NUMBERS THAT PROPHESY
THE MAN ON THE MOON AND APOLLO 11

11 – Comparing Apples and Oranges

In the Positive: Heroes Rising

In the Negative: Disorder

The number 11 has been a major progressive revelation to me through the years. It is very much connected to the revelation of the number 9, and also has two meanings.

Whereas 9 represents judgment, with the emphasis being that it is "by the Spirit," 11 represents judgment, with the emphasis being "disorder." It means disintegration or things falling apart. It's what happens when you add man (6) to the mix of God's perfect order (10) and when you fall short of God perfectly ruling over something (12). The number between those two is the number 11, which is a recipe for God's judgment to fall upon that disorder.

In the positive, 11 stands out as marking where God recognizes the faithfulness of people—a number associated with valor and notable acts of selfless service. This is the case for the prophetic type of the Apollo 11 crew.

When God is speaking something positive using the number 11, or showing what I call the "redeemed value," He likes to recognize victorious attributes of people. When people win huge battles of faith, He will stamp the number 11 on it. This number is associated with mighty deeds and extraordinary acts.

THE FAITH HALL OF FAME

The faith hall of fame is in Hebrews chapter 11. These world-class veterans overcame by faith, so that chapter is marked by 11. There are 19 people listed in Hebrews chapter 11.

VETERANS DAY

The day we celebrate our heroes who have battled for us in the United States is 11/11. World War I ended on the 11th hour of the 11th day of the 11th month. This is called Remembrance Day in the Common-wealth of Nations and parts of Europe.

GUN SALUTE

Eleven is the number of guns in a salute to the U.S. Army, Air Force, and Marine Corps Brigadier Generals and to Navy and Coast Guard Rear Admirals Lower Half.

A HERO RISES TO THE MOON

The first lunar landing was made by Apollo 11.

THE GREATEST HERO EVER

Jesus Christ was 33 years old when He conquered sin and death at the Cross. That is 11 x 3.

THE 11TH HOUR

The number 11 is also associated with urgency. The phrase "the 11th hour" suggests time running out or being at the very end of a time-line. Because the clock runs to 12, this is the last hour to get things done.

"The 11th hour" also refers to finality and the very end of time. It is associated with the promise that God will soon put the chaos in this world into perfect order.

It is no coincidence. It is, in fact, the very prophetic voice of Almighty God, at the beginning of this last century, declaring the ushering in of the end times through the 11s surrounding World War I.

Heroes Who Overcome Great Obstacles

In the book of Revelation, God's promises are only for those who overcome the end-time spirit of disorder that would rule before the King of kings comes back to clean house. It only makes sense that the word *overcometh* would appear in the Bible exactly 11 times. It is also no doubt significant that *overcome* would appear in the Bible 22 times (11 x 2).

Our God is incredibly good and tells us in His Word that He wants to do exceedingly, abundantly more than we can hope, ask, or imagine (see Ephesians 3:20 NIV). This major historic happening reminds us that listening to and following God's word is exciting so mankind can continue to explore and expand in ability, knowledge, and new frontiers as He leads us.

In the middle of this adventure, there were tremendous unknowns and some unforeseeable challenges. Rather than shrinking back and giving up, the men pressed on. God's Word says,

> *For God has not given us a spirit of fear, but of power and of love and of a sound mind* (2 Timothy 1:7 NKJV).

We have sound minds given to us by our Creator. If we give in to the spirit of fear, we often shut our minds down and don't react as well as we are programmed to do. Valor stirred up in the soul of man activates the supernatural power and sound mind of mankind that are provided by God who loves them.

NOTES

1 Colin Schultz, "The Moon Smells Like Gunpowder," *Smithsonian Magazine,* August 27, 2014; https://www.smithsonianmag.com/smart -news/moon-smells-gunpowder-180952494/; accessed December 14, 2023.

2 Elizabeth Howell, "Apollo 11 Moon Landing had a Plan for Lunar Germs—But Video Clip Reveals a Big Flaw," Space.com, July 6, 2019; https://www.space.com/pbs-chasing-the-moon-apollo-11-quarantine .html; accessed December 14, 2023.

3 Erin Blakemore, "Buzz Aldrin Took Holy Communion on the Moon. NASA Kept it Quiet," History.com, September 6, 2019; https:// www.history.com/news/buzz-aldrin-communion-apollo-11-nasa; accessed December 14, 2023.

4 Robin McKie, "How Michael Collins became the forgotten astronaut of Apollo 11," The Observer/The Guardian.com, July 19, 2009; https://www.theguardian.com/science/2009/jul/19/michael -collins-astronaut-apollo11; accessed December 14, 2023.

"I am responsible only to God and history."
—Francisco Franco

"God will use whatever He wants to display His glory. Heavens and stars. History and nations. People and problems."
—Max Lucado

"The aim of God in history is the creation of an all-inclusive community of loving persons with God Himself at the very heart of this community as its prime Sustainer and most glorious Inhabitant."
—Dallas Willard

4

PROPHETIC HISTORIC EVENT 4

THE SPACE SHUTTLE COLUMBIA

A plea from God for America to return to her first love.

Source: https://www.nasa.gov/
history/20-years-ago-remembering-columbia-and-her-crew

I think out of all the historic events included in this book, the disaster of the space shuttle Colombia is the hardest for me. I am a huge space exploration fan, and in my opinion the Columbia space shuttle crew for mission STS-107 was the finest assembly of explorative scientists ever put together.

Rick Husband, flight commander and fellow Texan, was not only at the top of his game in this astronaut business but was also someone who loved God with all of his heart. His life is truly amazing to me.

David Brown, Laurel Clark, Kalpana Chawla, Michael Anderson, William McCool, and Ilan Ramon were not only top-notch in their field but were some of the highest caliber people in character and heart on and above the planet Earth.

When this tragedy happened, I was shocked. Not at the reality of the dangers of reentry but at the potential "faith quake" of how something this bad could happen to people this good.

That's a point to the prophetic word in this thunderous event. Because this entire mission team represents the good people of the land Columbus found and the disastrous consequences of losing your first love. None of us are impervious to disaster no matter how good we are. The United States of America is not undefeatable.

Know that "type" is akin to parable—it is not literal, but figurative. This terrible thing happened to really good people. Remember the words of Jesus when talking of a tragedy in His day that killed some very good people and left the nation of Israel shocked and devastated:

> *Just at that time some people came who told Jesus about the Galileans whose blood Pilate [the governor] had mixed with their sacrifices. Jesus replied to them, "Do you think that these*

Galileans were worse sinners than all other Galileans because they have suffered in this way? I tell you, no; but unless you repent [change your old way of thinking, turn from your sinful ways and live changed lives], you will all likewise perish. Or do you assume that those eighteen on whom the tower in Siloam fell and killed were worse sinners than all the others who live in Jerusalem? I tell you, no; but unless you repent [change your old way of thinking, turn from your sinful ways and live changed lives], you will all likewise perish" (Luke 13:1-5 AMP).

We tend to think that judgment cannot happen to righteous people or at a place filled with good people. This, in itself, is a terrible assumption. Just as God causes rain to fall on both the righteous and unrighteous (Matthew 5:45), death comes to us all and so do the rules of judgment.

For since by man came death, by Man also came the resurrection of the dead. For as in Adam all die, even so in Christ all shall be made alive. But each one in his own order: Christ the firstfruits, afterward those who are Christ's at His coming (1 Corinthians 15:21-23 NKJV).

Yes, every one of us—saved or not, righteous or wicked—will someday die. We forget that death is the only way to eternal life with King Jesus, our Bridegroom, which is to make Him our first love by having a personal relationship with Him.

The prophetic word to America in this tragic event is that it can happen even though America has John Wayne, white picket fences, and Mickey Mouse. The magic of our nation has to deal with the humbling reality of seeing the blind spot that will kill us at the very end of our mission as a nation. Even if we are just 16 minutes from landing home.

PROPHETIC MESSAGE
PROPHETIC TYPE AND SHADOW

So I remind you that this is not literal, it is type. God uses very bad people to be the prophetic type and symbol of something very good and like that, incredibly good people can be the prophetic type of something that doesn't take part in God's Kingdom.

The prophetic interpretation of a type involves seeing a historical person, place, event, or institution as having a future historical fulfillment. It's just like interpreting a dream but this is done by seeing the people and the places as obvious symbols. Types are molds, templates, patterns, and examples of spiritual realities and things in the Kingdom.

This is reflected in the New Testament. The Greek word *týpos,* meaning "example," describes a model or pattern in the Old Testament that is fulfilled in the life and mission of Jesus Christ.

The Greek word *týpos* in the King James Version is also translated as "pattern" (Titus 2:7; Hebrews 8:5), "form" (Romans 6:17), "print" (John 20:25), "example" (1 Corinthians 10:11), "fashion" (Acts 7:44), "figure" (Acts 7:43; Romans 5:14), and "manner" (Acts 23:25).

So God prophetically uses natural events, people, and all forms of nouns to figuratively convey deep spiritual truth and reveal otherwise invisible messages. There is a voice within the thunder, but you have to know the language through the lens of God's Word.

IN THIS PROPHETIC SYMBOL AND TYPE: COLUMBIA IS AMERICA

The definition of the name Columbia looks like this: The United States or the land discovered by Christopher Columbus. This is why our nation's capital was named the District of Columbia. Columbia is the female personification of Columbus, which means "the dove"—a prophetic picture of being led or covered by the Holy Spirit.

THE NUMBERS THAT PROPHESY

FEBRUARY 1, 2003

The first of February was a day that America stood in silent shock. It was actually a really bad week for NASA altogether. On January 27, 1967, the Apollo 1 disaster happened. On January 28, 1986, the Challenger disaster happened, and the Colombia event happened all within the same calendar week. It was a bad day during a historically bad week.

What was there to say? President George W. Bush said it all in an AP televised address to the nation:

> My fellow Americans, this day has brought terrible news, and great sadness to our country. At 9 o'clock this morning, Mission Control in Houston lost contact with our Space Shuttle Columbia. A short time later, debris was seen falling from the skies above Texas. The Columbia is lost; there are no survivors.

It happened at 9 a.m. Exactly 9 a.m. to the literal second Central Standard Time.

In the sky 200,000 feet over Amarillo, Texas—exactly above where Commander Rick Husband and pilot William McCool spent their childhoods looking up at the stars—the orbiter Columbia began to disintegrate. At 18 seconds past the 9 o'clock hour, witnesses and videos could see the shuttle coming apart. Multiple ion trails streaked across the sky as hot metal entered the atmosphere at 16 times the speed of sound. The crew module stayed intact for 57 seconds, then broke into tiny pieces, killing all 7 crew members.

A Terrible Tragedy on a Beautiful Day

If you were around in 2003, less than two years after the American tragedy of 9/11/2001, you remember this day. As soon as I saw it on TV, I ran outside to my front yard and saw the ion trails scratching the blue sky above. I had no idea that debris was on its way down to the very real estate I was standing on. Four days later, a helmet and part of the body of one of these brave astronauts would be found a quarter mile from my tiny church in North Central Texas.

It was truly a catastrophe and the loss of some of the finest human beings our day, or any day, had ever seen. Again, the date was 2/1/03. I believe the pattern speaks of the plans of the enemy. How so? There is a famous saying by Vladimir Lenin, the enemy of the USA and freedom-loving people everywhere, that goes something like this: "It is necessary sometimes to take one step backward to take two steps forward."

It is a word on taking an intended loss to push your agenda ahead twice as far. One step backward from 2 and 2 steps forward from 1. From 2/1/3, there were 333 days remaining in the year 2003.

Call to Me and I will answer you, and tell you [and even show you] great and mighty things, [things which have been confined and hidden], which you do not know and understand and cannot distinguish (Jeremiah 33:3 AMP).

This was a 333 event and most folks completely missed the number that prophesies. God wanted us then, and still wants us now, to look up and cry out to Him. There is something He wants to tell us and show us—a dangerous blind spot.

There was a fatal hole in Columbia's protection they couldn't see. When Columbia took off on January 16, just 81 seconds into the flight, a piece of foam from the external fuel tank hit the left wing, leaving a huge hole in the heat-resistant panel protecting the shuttle and its crew.

Nobody noticed until the next day when the launch was being reviewed by experts. It got the attention of NASA's Inter-Center Photo investigators, and 3 days later, a Debris Assessment Team (DAT) reportedly requested images of the left wing.

They never got them.

According to the Accident Investigation Board, NASA official Linda Ham blocked all three image requests. The thought was it would waste too much time.

That's interesting to me because one of the last transmissions from Mission Control to Specialist Laurel Clark was to ask her to perform some small task. She replied that she was currently occupied but would get to it in a minute. "Don't worry about it," she was told. "You have all the time in the world."

AN INDESTRUCTIBLE PART OF THE WING

The chief engineers didn't believe foam could damage the part of the wing that was hit because it was reinforced and considered indestructible.

Ham would later explain she had no knowledge of the DAT's concerns, but the Debris Assessment Team had to rely on computer simulations to guess if the shuttle was still protected. They concluded the heat would cause damage, but not enough to cause major harm. They were wrong.

NASA informed Commander Rick Husband of the possible damage but informed him, "There is no concern."

This was truly a blind spot they could not imagine. A giant hole in part of their shield they thought was indestructible. They never saw it. Had they known, the space shuttle Atlantis, which was being prepared for take-off, could have rescued all 7 of the crew.

Studies of the takeoff would prove that the foam smashed the wing at 81 seconds. 9 x 9 = 81 and 8 + 1 = 9.

The number 9, in this case, certainly represents judgment. Remember, Colombia also disintegrated at exactly 9:00 a.m., at precisely that very second.

9 — THE NUMBER THAT PROPHESIES

- All forms of the word *death* appear 999 times in the Bible.

- There are 9 biblical sieges of Jerusalem.

- In Haggai chapter 1, God's judgment is poured out 9 times.

- Nine people are stoned to death in the Bible.

- There are 9 things in the book of Judges through which God does amazing miracles.

- The name Adam is found in the Bible 9 times.

- The phrase "my wrath" in the Greek, has a numeric value, gematria, of 999.

- There are 9 biblical situations when fire came down upon the earth from Heaven.

- There are 9 Supreme Court Justices in America.

66 AND THE ROUTE OF OUR JOURNEY

At the time of the foam strike during takeoff, the orbiter was at an altitude of about 66,000 feet. It's also interesting because Earth moves at 66,000 miles per hour on our yearlong course around the sun. I've noticed that the number 66 seems to be stamped upon things that represent *journey* or *traveling*. Route 66 here in the USA is a good example, as well as the 66-day journey of the Pilgrims on the Mayflower back in the year 1620.

A third of 66 is 22 and half of 66 is 33. The prime factors of 66 are 2 x 3 x 11.

Scientists say that it takes 66 days to replace a bad habit with a good one, and this I would call the road to recovery. Of course, the Bible has 66 books for our journey through life.

So I couldn't help but notice the prophetic numbers associated with the altitude and the speed the Columbia was traveling when the collision occurred. At that altitude, 66,000 feet, and 81 seconds after liftoff, Colombia was traveling at Mach 2.46.

The speed they were traveling at the time the foam struck matches the number of the word I believe God is using to warn America: *Mach 2.46.*

Yet I hold this against you: You have forsaken the love you had at first. Consider how far you have fallen! Repent and do the things you did at first. If you do not repent, I will come to you and remove your lampstand from its place. But you have this in your favor: You hate the practices of the Nicolaitans, which I also hate (Revelation 2:4-6 NIV).

THE CREW'S DESPERATE LAST MOMENTS

During the early morning hours of February 1, after a successful 16-day mission that began on January 16, STDS 107, led by Commander Rick Husband and copiloted by William McCool, began the return home.

At 8:44:09 a.m., Columbia reentered the atmosphere at a point called the entry interface. Four and a half minutes after entry interface, a sensor began recording greater-than-normal amounts of strain on the left wing. Something unusual was causing drag. It was picked up and recorded by the computer but not transmitted to the crew or ground controllers, so nobody knew.

Colombia began to veer toward the left, but this was not noticed by the crew or mission control because of corrections from the orbiter's flight control system. That means the boosters were going off automatically to correct and adjust.

Inside the cockpit, the bumps and noises were considered to be part of the violent reentry of Earth's atmosphere. Traveling at Mach 23, the wings' temperatures were at 2,800 degrees Fahrenheit and a bright orange glow was seen through the windows of Colombia.

At 8:53:46 a.m., Columbia crossed over the California coast. As soon as it entered American air space, several small pieces of the wing broke off and the glowing debris was seen from the ground.

Columbia continued its reentry and traveled over Utah, Arizona, New Mexico, and Texas, where most on board casually took video and waved at the camera, completely confident in the integrity of the spacecraft. Meanwhile, the observers looking up from Earth, would report seeing signs of debris being shed as big pieces came off glowing like shooting stars. They were coming apart and they didn't know it.

At 8:58:03 a.m., the orbiter's trim changed from the plan because of the increasing drag caused by the damage to the left wing.

At 8:58:21 a.m., the orbiter shed a Thermal Protection System (TPS) tile that landed in Littlefield, Texas—the western-most piece of recovered debris. A month later, the eastern-most piece of debris found was an 800-pound part of the engine, near Fort Polk, Louisiana.

At 8:58:39 a.m. the crew first became aware of a problem. Warning lights began to flash and show a loss of pressure in the tires of the left landing gear. Now this was inside the protected covering of the TPS and didn't make sense. What was actually happening was that the hole in their heat armor was causing hot gas to blow into the interior of the craft like a giant cutting torch. The plasma began to destroy and melt everything inside the wing, including the landing gear.

The pilot and commander then received indications that the status of the left landing gear was unknown and the sensors went out altogether.

The drag of the left wing continued to yaw the orbiter to the left until it could no longer be corrected using trim. The orbiter's Reaction Control System (RCS) thrusters began firing continuously to correct its orientation. It was trying hard not to go sideways. At that speed, going sideways would mean losing everything aerodynamic and the craft would shatter into a million pieces. They were traveling at 12,200 miles an hour—16 times faster than the speed of sound.

At 8:59:32 a.m., mission control stopped receiving information from the orbiter when Husband's last radio call of, "Roger, uh..." was cut off mid-transmission.

The flight data recorder found later in Palestine, Texas, revealed that one of the channels in the flight control software was bypassed as the result of a failed wire. They were trying to communicate when a master alarm began sounding on the flight deck.

What happened after that has been put together through investigative teams at NASA and released in a January 2009 report.

About 7 seconds after they lost communication, the master alarm went off. Failures throughout the ship filled the cabin with the noise of screaming alarms. Indicator lights went ablaze. The crew on the flight deck responded to these alarms in accordance with their training. Those seated on the mid deck prepared for anything and everything. Some scrambled to put their gloves and helmets on.

Then, the left wing buckled and either clung to the side of the ship or tore off altogether. The craft went into a violent spin to the left and the spin was so hard it broke all of the shoulder restraints to their seatbelts. The jolt was so hard it broke the helmets of some of the crew.

The Columbia then began to flip end over end, with the tail going into the wind. The hot plasma ignited the fuel in the rear engines and exploded in a violent blast, decapitating Colombia and separating the crew cabin from the spaceship.

They lost cabin pressure, and at 200,000 feet the force must have been indescribable. Those still conscious closed their visors when cabin pressure was lost. Their suits automatically pressurized. It was now only a question of hoping that the cabin held together until it fell low enough—below 40,000 feet or so—for them to blow the escape hatch and jump free. This was not an entirely hopeless situation, until the cabin's own structure began to fail.

At 9:00:05 a.m. the autopilot switch was turned on and the hydraulic systems switch was hit to restore. It failed. Either Husband or McCool was still conscious and trying to regain control.

At 9:00:18 a.m., Colombia began to totally disintegrate, and all onboard computer recording stopped. Ground observers noted a sudden increase in debris being shed, and all onboard systems lost power.

9:00:35 a.m. The pieces of the orbiter continued to break apart into smaller pieces, and within a minute after breakup, were too small to be detected from ground-based videos.

For the next 35 minutes Colombia fell from the sky.

By 9:35 a.m., all debris and crew's remains were estimated to have impacted the ground.

At the very time Colombia was supposed to be landing in Florida, families on the ground began to hear reports of people in Texas saying they had seen it break apart in the skies above them.

They were 16 minutes from home.

Traveling at Mach 16 after a 16-day mission that started on the 16th of January.

They were 16 minutes short of home.

The Prophetic Warning: America, you are blind to the fact that you are not protected.

Just like Samson, the disaster of Colombia illustrates that America thinks it will always work the way it always has worked, not knowing that the Spirit of God will no longer protect us.

> *And she said, "The Philistines are upon you, Samson!" So he awoke from his sleep, and said, "I will go out as before, at other times, and shake myself free!" But he did not know that the Lord had departed from him* (Judges 16:20 NKJV).

Why? What is the warning telling us to turn from? It's all about the first thing remaining the first thing—or facing a disaster at the end of our mission.

FIRSTS

Columbia was all about "the first thing":

- Columbia was the first of the shuttles built and the first into space.

- Israel's first astronaut and payload specialist, Ilan Ramon, was aboard. It was his first time in space.

- Mission Specialist Kalpana Chawla was the first person of Indian descent in space.

- It was Commander Rick Husband's first time to command a shuttle mission.

- Pilot William McCool's first time in space.

- Mission Specialist Laurel Clark's first time in space.

- Mission Specialist David Brown's first time in space.

- The first disaster in the history of NASA that happened while reentering the atmosphere.

- It was the first trip in three years dedicated to science.

- It was the first time NASA used a research double module to conduct experiments.

- There were a total of 88 first-time experiments conducted on the mission.

- The Columbia disaster happened on the first of February.

- At the memorial service, President Bush arrived with astronauts Neil Armstrong (the first man on the moon) and John Glenn (the first astronaut to orbit Earth).

The name "Columbia" seems to be associated with a lot of firsts, including:

- The first privately owned American ship to circumnavigate the globe was named Columbia. It set sail from Boston commanded by Robert Gray on May 11, 1792. She was the first American ship to visit the west coast of North America, the first American ship to land in the Hawaiian Islands, and the first American ship to circumnavigate the globe.

- The first USS Columbia of the United States Navy was a three-masted, wooden-hulled sailing frigate. It was one of the first US naval ships to circumnavigate the globe.

- SS Columbia (1880-1907) was the first ship to carry a dynamo powering electric lights instead of oil lamps. It was also the first commercial use of electric light bulbs outside of Thomas Edison's

Menlo Park, New Jersey, laboratory. It's interesting that the SS Columbia was lost on July 21, 1907, after a collision with the lumber schooner off Shelter Cove, California, with the loss of 88 lives. The space shuttle Colombia was lost, as we know, with 88 official NASA experiments on board.

What is the first thing?

> *"Teacher, which is the great commandment in the law?" Jesus said to him, "'You shall love the Lord your God with all your heart, with all your soul, and with all your mind.'* **This is the first and great commandment**" (Matthew 22:36-38 NKJV).

We know that the first thing we can't lose is our love for God, and 16 is the biblical number for "the love of God."

THE NUMBER 16 AND THE COLUMBIA

- Columbia left Earth on January 16.

- It was in space for 16 days.

- They were 16 minutes from home when disaster struck.

- Columbia was scheduled to land in Florida at 9:16 EST.

- They were traveling at Mach 16 when the spaceship and crew disintegrated.

- While Israel's first astronaut, Ilan Ramon, was facing death, the election of the 16th Knesset was taking place in Israel at exactly this time.

SWEET 16 AND THE NUMBER THAT PROPHESIES LOVE

Biblically, 16 represents love—expressly, the love of God.

- There are 16 attributes of love found in "The Love Chapter" (1 Corinthians 13).

- There are 16 baptisms throughout the Word of God.

- There are 16 commands given to the nation of Israel.

- Acts 15:25 is the 16th time Paul's name is mentioned, and he is called "beloved."

- There are 16 Jehovah titles.

- Lincoln was the 16th president; and in the Kingdom, 16 is when you lay down your life for the love of God.

  Greater love hath no man than this, that a man lay down his life for his friends (John 15:13 KJV).

Lincoln lost his life for his friends.

SEVEN STARS

Seven "stars" are representative of the 7 churches mentioned in Revelation 1:20–3:22.

George W. Bush, 43rd President of the United States, declared after the Columbia tragedy: "The same Creator that named the stars also knows the names of the 7 souls we name today."

These 7 astronauts have been called the "7 stars" over and over again.

The wife of Israeli astronaut Ilam Ramon is famous for saying that he loved the stars so much, "and now he has become one."

THE SEVEN STARS AND THE WARNING IN REVELATION

There is a hidden message in the date of the Columbia disaster—February 2, 2003, or 2/01/03—and you can find this message in Revelation 2:1-3. Let's search out the matter one verse at a time:

> *To the angel of the church of Ephesus write, "These things says He who holds the **seven stars** in His right hand, who walks in the midst of the seven golden lampstands"* (Revelation 2:1 NKJV).

Remember, I told you that Columbia is symbolic for the United States. Therefore, this word has to do with our nation. Also, keep in mind the 7 brave souls of the flight crew, above our heads in the firmament called Heaven (Genesis 1:7-8), streaking through the sky as points of light—falling stars—as they re-entered Earth's atmosphere. Their lives, and for certain their shocking deaths, lampstands to illuminate both the positive and the negative of our nation's spiritual heart:

> *I know your works, your labor, your patience, and that you cannot bear those who are evil. And you have tested those who say they are apostles and are not, and have found them liars* (Revelation 2:2 NKJV).

> *And you have persevered and have patience, and have labored for My name's sake and have not become weary* (Revelation 2:3 NKJV).

God is pleased with the good works, generosity, and kindness of the American people and the church. He recognizes it, but we find it's not enough. I wish the Scripture text stopped there, but it doesn't.

> *Nevertheless I have this against you, that you have left your first love* (Revelation 2:4 NKJV).

Remember, Columbia is marked with firsts and sixteens—first love.

> *Remember therefore from where you have fallen; repent and do the first works, or else I will come to you quickly and remove your lampstand from its place—unless you repent* (Revelation 2:5 NKJV).

The candlestick is the Lord's manifest presence and protection.

You don't get the benefit of the candlestick if you refuse to be the place of light to a world in darkness. We need to remember from where we have fallen in this parable, and it's all about the first love.

The commander of STS 107 was Rick ("brave ruler") Husband. The word *husband* speaks of "covenant love." It speaks of Jesus, indeed a brave Ruler who refers to Himself in Scripture as "the Bridegroom"— the husband—and us as His bride.

And it used to be that as a nation, we were submitted to and in covenant with God Almighty. What's real is we don't love Him anymore. Just like Columbia, as it reentered the atmosphere, we have taken control of our nation away from our Husband, and now we trust in our technology.

Too many of us love our Starbucks, our iPhones, Netflix, and posting our opinions on Facebook. And too many love the Kardashians, Pokémon Go, Squid Game, and really anything that is anti-Jesus, or as the apostle John puts it in 1 John 4:1, *"false prophets."*

The Columbia crew was destroyed because there was a split in the protective covering. This caused Columbia to turn left when it should have gone straight. At 16 times the speed of sound, aerodynamically, it was destined to break into 10,000 pieces.

"Their mission was almost complete and we lost them so close to home," President Bush said. He said they were only minutes away from arrival and reunion. Sixteen minutes from home to be exact. So what is the message to the church of Ephesus that is also being prophesied to you, me, and America today?

We are so close to the end. Let's not lose it now! Return, Colombia, to your first love. Remember your covenant love and the One who commands you. Remember from where you have fallen. You're leaning to the left, and it's going to be disastrous! Your wing has a hole in it!

THE SHADOW OF HIS WINGS

Wings represent flight; but in the Bible they also represent a holy protective covering and our trust that we are protected.

> *The Lord repay your work, and a full reward be given you of the Lord God of Israel, under whose wings you have come for refuge* (Ruth 2:12 NKJV).

> *Keep me as the apple of Your eye; hide me under the shadow of Your wings* (Psalm 17:8 NKJV).

I will abide in Your tabernacle forever; I will trust in the shelter of Your wings (Psalm 61:4 NKJV).

He shall cover you with His feathers, and under His wings shall you take refuge; His truth shall be your shield and buckler (Psalm 91:4 NKJV).

If you had a dream that there was a massive hole in your left wing that you didn't know about, it would mean that you think you are protected and you're not. While leaning to the left *politically* means a tendency to be liberal or socialist/humanist, but leaning to the left *prophetically* means leaning toward weakness and away from strength. In this case, both apply.

SUMMARY FACTS
NUMBERS THAT PROPHESY IN CONTEXT

- 9: (+) Fruit bearing or (–) Judgment over death
- 18: (+) Life or (-) Bondage
- 7: Fullness, completion, end of a timeline
- 13: Rebellion
- 16: The love of God
- 333: Calling out to God
- 107: Being found (Perfect)
- 28: Times and seasons

Consider These Prophetic Pictures of the Disaster:

- "Colombia" means "The land discovered by Columbus" and represents America.

- The Commander of America (Columbia) is our Husband (Rick Husband).

- The flight recorder was found in Palestine, Texas. (Palestine is the enemy of God's chosen people.)

- The NASA official Linda Ham blocked all three image requests. The descendants of Hamm are biblically cursed and fall into the category of the enemies of God's people, the Canaanites (Genesis 9:24-27).

- The NASA flight director, again an amazing human being but a symbolic type in this parable, was LeRoy Cain. Cain is of course the firstborn son of Adam and Eve and the murderer of his brother Abel.

- All the firsts with Colombia and all the sixteens with this mission speak of "First Love."

- They were at speed Mach 2.46 when the foam punched a hole in the wing during takeoff. Revelation 2:4-6 (NIV) says, *"Yet I hold this against you: You have forsaken the love you had at first. Consider how far you have fallen! Repent and do the things you did at first. If you do not repent, I will come to you and remove your lampstand from its place. But you have this in your favor: You hate the practices of the Nicolaitans, which I also hate."*

- The foam strike happened at 81 seconds. 9 x 9 = 81 Judgment. 8 + 1 = 9 Judgment.

- The Colombia broke apart at exact 9:00 a.m. Judgment.

- They couldn't see that their protection was damaged and they were vulnerable; everyone thought the damaged part of the wing was impenetrable.

- On February 1 there were 333 days remaining in the year. Jeremiah 33:3 says that if we will call out to God, He will show us things we don't know.

- The 7 astronauts were called the "7 stars" and they represent the church in the book of Revelation.

- The date was 2-1-3. Revelation 2:1-3 is the address of King Jesus to the church of Ephesus also known as the church who lost her first love.

- Moments before the disintegration, ground control said, "You have all the time in the world." It wasn't true then—and it isn't true now.

In trying to determine the survivability of this scenario, NASA said, "There is no known complete protection from the breakup event except to prevent its occurrence."

It's up to the United States of America to prevent this occurrence. Otherwise, no matter how fine the people are on board, even God's chosen people (the first Israeli in space) will face certain disaster.

"In Him (God), history and prophecy are one and the same."
—Aiden Wilson Tozer

*"God acts in history: that is, God provides ideas, methods, and
experiences intended to bring comprehension to man,
an understanding heart, a conscious life."*
—Jacob Needleman

"He who has ears to hear, let him hear!"
—Jesus Christ, Son of God, Matthew 11:15 NKJV

5

PROPHETIC HISTORIC EVENT 5

PRINCESS DIANA AND MOTHER TERESA

The near-simultaneous deaths of Princess Diana and Mother Teresa

Source: https://commons.wikimedia.org/wiki/File:Kay_Kelly_of_Liverpool_%26_Mother_Teresa_in_1980_(cropped).jpg; https://commons.wikimedia.org/wiki/File:Diana,_Princess_of_Wales.jpg

If you are like many, you probably remember where you were when you heard of the car wreck that ended the life of the "People's Princess," Princess Diana. The beautiful Lady Di had captured hearts around the world as her life was constantly sent forth by relentless cameras as their flashes of light brought her into focus for us all.

Five days later, an equally beautiful soul, Mother Teresa, passed quietly from her earthly life with far less media coverage. She walked in the darkest places, bringing enlightenment with no fanfare or glamour.

These two strikingly different lives give us easy-to-find prophetic symbols. So easy that it is hard to miss the voice within the thunder in the near-simultaneous deaths of Princess Diana and Mother Teresa. They were both incredible women with profound worldwide influence. The circumstances of their deaths are symbols that offer two opposing scenarios. What the numbers prophesy are dramatic wonders that parallel the dramatic wonders of their lives, deaths, and legacies.

The story of Princess Diana's death at age 36 in a catastrophic crash in a Paris traffic tunnel continues to shock us all these decades later. Did you know the car she was traveling in hit the 13th pillar in the Pont de l'Alma tunnel? The early reports that day said the tunnel was 666 feet long. The speedometer was stuck on 120 mph, so yes, there was a huge crash—an explosion that quickly reverberated around the world.

For a few minutes in the dark night, there was the blare of a car horn set off by the driver's slumped body, and then the clicking of camera shutters by the swarm of paparazzi she was desperate to avoid. The "paparazzi" lived up to the meaning of the word as they sought her with the persistence of hungry flies.

August 31, 1997, in Paris, the City of Light, Princess Diana left the Ritz Carlton seeking privacy and perhaps peace to instead encounter sickening fear, trauma, and then tragically, her death in a dark tunnel.

Five days later, in Calcutta where the poorest of India's poor live, in a convent she built, Mother Teresa was surrounded by grieving nuns when she breathed her last breath and moved peacefully into Heaven.

Remember, this is type and symbol, and the message is like reading straight out of the Bible. The humanity is heartbreaking, the drama is captivating, and the Word from the Lord is undeniable to those who fear the Lord. Friend, we all need to hear this word—these are types, symbols, and numbers that prophesy to us now.

Anyone with ears to hear should listen and understand! (Matthew 11:15 NLT)

PROPHETIC MESSAGE

Two Women, Two Prophetic Symbols

Using our prophetic eyes, we see that in the prophetic picture, we have two ladies who represent the church as different symbols. Let's look at Mother Teresa first.

THE NUMBERS THAT PROPHESY

MOTHER TERESA AND THE MARK OF GRACE

Mother Teresa was not just a person. She was a type and a symbol in our generation. Her selflessness affected our very culture, and she became a worldwide symbol of grace and virtue.

When one speaks derogatorily of another, we might say, "She is no Mother Teresa." Or we might throw that name out in another way here or there, but instantly, you know what her name represents.

The number 5 speaks of the Grace of God. It also has to do with the favor of God. The number 5 marks the place where God gives us the ability to overcome something. Mother Teresa's life is marked by the number 5.

Consider some examples of the number 5 associated with her life, and remember: 5 is grace, and grace is God's ability to overcome.

- On October 7, 1950, Mother Teresa received permission from the Vatican in Rome to start her own order, The Missionaries of Charity. Their primary task was to love and care for those persons whom no one was prepared to look after, especially lepers and those with AIDS.

- In the 5th month in 1931, Agnes Gonxha Bojaxhiu took her first vows as a nun and received a new name: Teresa.

- In 1952, she founded the Nirmal Hriday (Pure Heart) Home for the Dying, in a former Hindu temple in Calcutta.

- In 1979, Mother Teresa received the Nobel Peace Prize—the 5th of 5 Nobel Prizes.

- In 1985, she received the Presidential Medal of Freedom. It was President Reagan's 5th presentation of that medal.

- In 1996, she was the 5th person ever to be made an honorary citizen of the United States, following Winston Churchill, William Penn, Hannah Penn, and Raoul Wallenberg.

- Mother Teresa died September 5, 1997—5 days after the death of Prince Diana shocked the world.

- The funeral was held at the 15,000-seat Netaji Indoor Stadium.

- Mother Teresa's order has more than 500 missions throughout 100 countries.

Mother Teresa was and still is a symbol of selfless service to both people and God. She was known to have great love for people: *"By this all will know that you are My disciples, if you have love for one another"* (John 13:35 NKJV).

Therefore, Mother Teresa represents a disciple of Christ; and as a nun, she symbolizes the bride of Christ.

Sometimes I get criticized because I don't say things just to please other people. Neither did Mother Teresa. Once when talking to the nuns at her convent, she said, "If you don't have zeal to help the poor, to take care of the leper, you should pack up and go home, for you have no reason to stay."

> [Jesus] *gave Himself for us, that He might redeem us from every lawless deed and purify for Himself His own special people, zealous for good works* (Titus 2:14 NKJV).

I remember seeing this headline: "Mother Teresa, Friend to the Lowliest Dies." That same headline would describe how Jesus lived while He walked the earth. He waded into a sea of human beings, moved among them, met them where they were, loved them fiercely, and touched and healed them all.

In some situations where Leanna and I travel to bring Jesus to hurting people all around the globe, we see things that are hard to see and hard to deal with. I have called it a terrible privilege to serve there. It is terrible to see the circumstances, but it is a privilege to be trusted by Jesus to go there and serve the people living there. Mother Teresa served with that same privilege.

> *Take My yoke upon you and learn from Me, for I am gentle and lowly in heart, and you will find rest for your souls* (Matthew 11:29 NKJV).

OBEDIENT FRIEND OF JESUS

Mother Teresa was an example of what Jesus says in John 15:

> *Greater love has no one than this: to lay down one's life for one's friends. You are my friends if you do what I command* (John 15:13-14 NIV).

She said, "I realized that I had a call to take care of the sick and the dying, the hungry, the naked, and the homeless to be God's love in action to the poorest of people."

PEACEMAKER

In 1979, Mother Teresa received the Nobel Peace Prize, recognizing her lifetime of humanitarian work caring for the sick and poor and establishing centers for the blind, aged, disabled, and dying, as well as a leper colony.

She never saw it as a personal achievement because she didn't operate from self-centeredness. During her Nobel Peace Prize acceptance speech, she said:

> ...To this love for one another and today when I have received this reward, I personally am most unworthy, and I having avowed poverty to be able to understand the poor, I

choose the poverty of our poor people. But I am grateful and I am very happy to receive it in the name of the hungry, of the naked, of the homeless, of the crippled, of the blind, of the lepers, of all those people who feel unwanted, unloved, uncared, thrown away of the society, people who have become a burden to society, and are ashamed by everybody. ...And let us all join in that one prayer, God give us courage to protect the unborn child, for the child is the greatest gift of God to a family, to a nation and to the whole world. God bless you![1]

SYMBOLS OF FREEDOM

In 1985, US President Ronald Reagan presented Mother Teresa with the Medal of Freedom, the highest US civilian award. Portions of his remarks:

A month ago, we awarded the Medal of Freedom to 13 heroes who have done their country proud. Only one of the recipients could not attend because she had work to do— not special work, not unusual work for her, but everyday work which is both special and urgent in its own right. Mother Teresa was busy saving the world. And I mean that quite literally. ...I believe Mother Teresa might point out that she is not an American but a daughter of Yugoslavia, and she has not spent her adult life in this country but in India. However...we honor her that the goodness in some hearts transcends all borders and all narrow nationalistic considerations. Some people, some very few people are, in the truest sense, citizens of the world; Mother Teresa is.[2]

In 1996, US President Bill Clinton conferred honorary United States citizenship on Mother Teresa, saying, "To be an American citizen is to share certain fundamental values: That we have a duty to help others live up to their God-given promise, that we have a responsibility to build up and reinforce the bonds of community, that we have an obligation to extend our hands to those who cannot always help themselves. By this measure, Mother Teresa is already an American citizen. I am proud to make it official."[3] Mother Teresa is the 5th person awarded this honor out of only eight people ever honored with US citizenship.

> *Now the Lord is the Spirit, and where the Spirit of the Lord is, there is liberty [emancipation from bondage, true freedom]* (2 Corinthians 3:17 AMP).

> *But now they desire a better, that is, a heavenly country. Therefore God is not ashamed to be called their God, for He has prepared a city for them* (Hebrews 11:16 NKJV).

BELOVED LEGACY

Upon learning of Mother Teresa's passing, Pope John Paul II said, "She was a glowing example of how the love of God can be transformed into love of one's neighbor."

US President Clinton said, "She led by serving, and she showed us the stunning power of humility."

Mother Teresa died on Friday, September 5, 1997, at the age of 87. After preaching a small evening service, she laid down in her bed in the monastery she had built 50 years earlier, and she died surrounded by devoted nuns.

History between the two women:

> The news of Mother Teresa's death came to some Indians as
> they watched late-night broadcasts from London about the
> late Princess Diana. Diana and Mother Teresa met for the
> first time in 1992 at the order's convent in Rome, and again
> in New York two months ago. Mother Teresa had planned
> for the order's nuns to say special prayers for Diana Saturday
> morning.
>
> L.M. Singhvi, India's ambassador in London, recalled in
> a BBC interview how Diana had gone to Calcutta this
> summer to see Mother Teresa but had missed her because
> the nun was in Rome, gravely ill. Diana still paid a visit to
> her Calcutta operations.
>
> "I said to [Diana], 'It is good you have seen her work before
> you've seen her,'" Singhvi said.
>
> "I think India has lost one of the greatest jewels in her
> crown.... She was the greatest jewel in that crown," he said.[4]

After Mother Teresa's body lay in state at Saint Thomas Church for
6 days, hundreds of thousands of mourners lined the procession route
to pay their last respects. Then, more than 15,000 attended the funeral
Mass, including 400 foreign delegates from two dozen countries, pres-
idents and prime ministers, and First Lady Hillary Clinton; there was
an international audience of millions.

From humble beginnings, the order she founded in 1950—the
Order of the Missionaries of Charity—at the time of her death

included hundreds of humanitarian centers in more than 123 countries with about 4,000 nuns and hundreds of thousands of lay workers. On September 4, 2016, in a ceremony witnessed by tens of thousands of people, including 1,500 homeless people from across Italy, Mother Teresa was canonized by Pope Francis as Saint Teresa of Calcutta.

> *"Teacher, which is the great commandment in the law?" Jesus said to him, "'You shall love the Lord your God with all your heart, with all your soul, and with all your mind.' This is the first and great commandment. And the second is like it: 'You shall love your neighbor as yourself'"* (Matthew 22:36-39 NKJV).

THE NUMBERS THAT PROPHESY
PRINCESS DIANA AND THE MARK OF THE WORLD

In the prophetic parable, Lady Diana is a symbol of the worldly church.

Diana bears the same name as the Roman goddess who watched over nature for both humans and animals. The goddess was the patron deity of wild animals, protecting them from ruthless treatment and regulating the rules of hunting activities for humans. She was considered the great mother image and gave fertility to humankind. Her temple was in Ephesus and is one of the 7 ancient wonders of the world.

Princess Diana is known to be one of the most photographed women in the history of photography because of her gentle beauty and royal status.

In Acts 19:23-41, the Bible records an incredible reference to the many images of the goddess Diana. Paul and his Jewish companions were making a great difference for the Kingdom in Ephesus. So many Ephesians were being converted to Christianity that the sale of silver idols or images dropped like bitcoin in 2021.

To the church that is loved by the world, considered beautiful and well-favored, God says, I see you.

> *Charm is deceptive, and beauty is fleeting; but a woman who fears the Lord is to be praised* (Proverbs 31:30 NIV).

"WHATEVER LOVE MEANS"

The year 1981 was a different world from our current world.

That was the year the space shuttle program began, and the Colombia roared her mighty engines for the first time. The Boeing 767 airliner made its first flight. The Centers for Disease Control in the United States reported that 5 homosexual men in Los Angeles had a rare form of pneumonia; which we would later call AIDS. MTV was launched in the US and aired its first video, "Video Killed the Radio Star" by The Buggles.

Cable TV meant people were watching more TV and had a greater variety of entertaining interests. And just like that, a beautiful 19-year-old British woman named Lady Spencer had everyone's attention.

Diana was announcing her engagement to the Prince of Wales, which meant she would one day be queen. "We had this ghastly interview the day we announced our engagement," she later said.

In a cringing moment for all the world to see, this teenage girl clung hard to her 32-year-old fiancé. Diana would write later, "And this ridiculous reporter said, 'Are you in love?' I thought, what a thick question. So I said, 'Yes, of course, we are,' and Charles turned round and said, 'Whatever love means.'"⁵

No one had blinked at his comment about having had his eye on her since she was 16, but you could feel something really bad and see it on her face when his declaration of love toward her was "whatever love means."

"It traumatized me," the young woman said.

I think that this is so prophetic of the word coming from this scenario. Diana's life was a constant redefinition of "whatever love means." In the actual interview, Charles added that the phrase "in love" is open to "your own interpretation."

FAST-FORWARD

Over the next 15 years, their troubled marriage, heartbreak, and betrayal of one another would be seen worldwide through the never-ending flashes of light bulbs and an ever-growing number of camera lenses focused on her. It was a sickening, continual harassment, and Diana's life in the royal family closely resembled the appalling crash that took her life on August 31, 1997.

Princess Diana and Prince Charles separated in 1992 and divorced in 1996. Her relationship with Dodi Al Fayed, a very rich, 42-year-old Egyptian, had become worldwide news in 1997. She flaunted this relationship for the press as they were seen about town, on his $300 million yacht, and in various high-profile places. They apparently were very serious about their relationship.

The day before their death, Fayed's sister told reporters that the couple planned to stay together and were possibly heading for marriage. And Adnan Khashoggi, Dodi Fayed's uncle and Saudi tycoon, told the press again on Friday, the day before they both died, "We welcome Diana into our family."

On that Saturday night, just moments before her death, she gave Fayed a pair of her father's cufflinks as a gift. This was a precious gift to her from her father.

By now, you have probably seen the haunting pictures of Diana and Dodi leaving through the back door of the Ritz in Paris and driving away. And you probably know that they were chased by the "paparazzi" into a tunnel, where the car crashed seconds after entering the 666-foot-long tunnel. The car went out of control, striking the 13th concrete pillar and careening into another wall.

The tunnel and the pillar are God's voice in the thunder.

666 – The complete length of the tunnel in the early reports. This means complete flesh.

This is the "mark of the beast." An animal, or a beast, has no concept of God. Spiritual and moral values are of no meaning to it. The number 6 represents man without God. The number 666 means "man, man, man" or "flesh, flesh, flesh." The tribulation world system will be totally man-centered, man-dominated, and man-subjugated. Everything in it will be based on man's animalistic thoughts, plans, actions, and schemes. There is no room for God in 666. People will be total flesh and that's why everyone is forced to wear the mark. When a number appears 3 times, it implies perfect completion of what that number represents, and 6 represents man or flesh.

Here is wisdom. Let him that hath understanding count the number of the beast: for it is the number of a man; and his number is Six hundred threescore and six (Revelation 13:18 KJV).

The later reports listed the tunnel as having a length of 153 meters, which converts to 501 feet. When you take the total of those numbers 5 + 0 + 1, the result is 6 and is a prophetic mark for flesh.

13 – *The 13th pillar where the car crashed = Rebellion*

Thirteen is the number most closely associated with apostasy. Apostasy is a fancy term used for something that once had the truth but lost it. Anytime you rebel against God, you lose. In fact, you lose everything.

When God wants to illustrate rebellion, whether it's against Him or even righteous rebellion against the world, He reaches for the number 13 to preach His great sermon.

The number 13 is attached to spiritual rebellion. If you really want to see rebellion illustrated biblically through the number 13, you need look no further than the 13 words in the 13th verse of the 13th chapter of the very first book of the Bible:

> *But the men of Sodom were wicked and sinners before the Lord exceedingly* (Genesis 13:13 KJV).

The word "rebel" is found in 13 verses throughout the Bible. I think it is worth noting that Nimrod, a name that means "rebel," was the founder of Babylon and all world religions and is the 13th descendant of Adam.

Frank Levi, the only known eyewitness to the actual crash other than paparazzi members, was driving ahead of the black Mercedes where Diana and Dodi were seated in the back seat. Through Levi's rearview mirror, he says he saw a motorcycle cut in front of the car, then a blinding flash from a camera, and then the car veering out of control.

The first ones at the crash were the pursuing paparazzi, snapping picture after picture as Diana lay pinned and dying in a mangled heap of crushed metal.

The word "paparazzi" means flies; one of satan's titles is "lord of the flies." There is no doubt that the tormentors were directly involved in her death, as proven by the jury verdict in 2008.[6]

After emergency surgery and two hours of heart massages from the surgeon on staff, Diana died at 6:00 a.m. Paris time; it was announced to the world in a Paris press conference. That day, the whole world mourned. It was reported that 2.5 billion people watched her funeral.

DIANA—A TYPE OF THE CHURCH MARKED BY THE WORLD

- Leaves her royal husband and flaunts her courtship with Egypt (the enemy of God).

- Gives her father's gifts away.

- Dines in the spotlight but leaves in the dark.

- Flees pursuing torment, but God says it is to no avail.

- God has a word for this church, and it is seen in the 13th pillar!

- Rebellion and righteousness do not mix; it means death for those who meet there!

Beware: If you think you can live off the royalty you have divorced yourself from and from the promotion of other people's righteousness, you will see an untimely end.

DIANA'S FUNERAL

Diana's funeral was called a "unique funeral for a unique lady." For example, her friend Elton John sang a song he had written for Marilyn Monroe's funeral, who also passed away at age 36. The song is titled "Candle in the Wind." Let's look at a few of the lyrics and the significance of the candle, the Spirit, and the presence of God in reflection of Revelation 2:4-6:

> And it seems to me you lived your life
> Like a candle in the wind
> Never knowing who to cling to
> When the rain set in
> Loneliness was tough
> The toughest role you ever played
> Your candle burned out long before
> Your legend ever did.
> —"Candle in the Wind," Elton John, 1973

Unto the church at Ephesus (Ephesus is the place of the temple of Diana):

> *But I have this [charge] against you, that you have left your first love [you have lost the depth of love that you first had for Me]. So remember the heights from which you have fallen, and repent [change your inner self—your old way of thinking, your sinful behavior—seek God's will] and do the works you did at first [when you first knew Me]; otherwise, I will visit you and remove your lampstand (the church, its impact) from its place—unless you repent. Yet you have this [to your*

credit], that you hate the works and corrupt teachings of the Nicolaitans [that mislead and delude the people], which I also hate (Revelation 2:4-6 AMP).

How tragic. Diana:

- had so much left to accomplish

- had children who needed her

- was killed while trying to protect her privacy

Mother Teresa said of Diana when she heard she had died, "Diana told me that if it were not for her position in the world, she would have come to work with us." Although this quote can't be substantiated, the prophetic conversation between Jesus and the rich young man in Luke 18:18-30 (NLT) comes to mind:

Once a religious leader asked Jesus this question: "Good Teacher, what should I do to inherit eternal life?"

"Why do you call me good?" Jesus asked him. "Only God is truly good. But to answer your question, you know the commandments: 'You must not commit adultery. You must not murder. You must not steal. You must not testify falsely. Honor your father and mother.'"

The man replied, "I've obeyed all these commandments since I was young."

When Jesus heard his answer, he said, "There is still one thing you haven't done. Sell all your possessions and give the money to the poor, and you will have treasure in heaven. Then come, follow me."

But when the man heard this he became very sad, for he was very rich.

When Jesus saw this, he said, "How hard it is for the rich to enter the Kingdom of God! In fact, it is easier for a camel to go through the eye of a needle than for a rich person to enter the Kingdom of God!"

Those who heard this said, "Then who in the world can be saved?"

He replied, "What is impossible for people is possible with God."

Peter said, "We've left our homes to follow you."

"Yes," Jesus replied, "and I assure you that everyone who has given up house or wife or brothers or parents or children, for the sake of the Kingdom of God, will be repaid many times over in this life, and will have eternal life in the world to come."

Perhaps the fine art of balancing the news coverage in such an extraordinary week would tax even the most thoughtful of television executives. Too much for Diana? Too little for Mother Teresa? It's difficult to say. And who knows if Mother Teresa herself might not have enjoyed the timing.

Recently a friend remarked how upset she was that Mother Teresa had died so shortly after Diana. "What horrible timing!"

she said, articulating the same reaction I had heard from a number of Catholics. "Now no one will notice!" But here, after all, was a woman who spent her life among the unnoticed, worked for decades in anonymity, shunned honors, and said that she was "personally unworthy" of the Nobel Prize. So it was comforting to think that dying at a time that almost ensured she would receive as little attention as possible, while frustrating for her many admirers, might have pleased Mother Teresa immensely.[7]

SUMMARY FACTS

MOTHER TERESA—A TYPE OF THE CHURCH MARKED BY GRACE

- Marked by grace in the way she lived.

- Served like Jesus as she ministered His love to the lowliest.

- Had no self-serving motives.

- Increased places to serve people with great needs.

- Refused accolades and pointed them to the purpose of His church.

PRINCESS DIANA—A TYPE OF THE CHURCH MARKED BY THE WORLD

- Leaves her royal husband and flaunts her courtship with Egypt (the enemy of God).

- Gives her father's gifts away.

- Dines in the spotlight but leaves in the dark.

- Flees pursuing torment, but God says it is to no avail.

- God has a word for this church, and it is seen in the 13th pillar!

- Rebellion and righteousness do not mix; it means death for those who meet there!

Beware: If you think you can live off the royalty you have divorced yourself from and from the promotion of other people's righteousness, you will see an untimely end.

It is very unfortunate that churches can't do the work that God has called them to do because people value their position in the world more than fulfilling their God-given calling.

What separates the violent demise of Princess Diana and the victorious place of rest of Mother Teresa? There is a span of 5 days, but more importantly, there is a chasm between the worldly human heart and the heartbeat of God. As God says through Jeremiah:

The heart is deceitful above all things and beyond cure. Who can understand it? I the Lord search the heart and examine the mind, to reward each person according to their conduct, according to what their deeds deserve. Like a partridge that hatches eggs it did not lay are those who gain riches by unjust means. When their lives are half gone, their riches will desert them, and in the end they will prove to be fools (Jeremiah 17:9-11 NIV).

At the time of Diana's tragic death, Mother Teresa said, "The most terrible poverty is loneliness and the feeling of being unloved."

Those words echo through the years and point the church to align with God the Father's love for all peoples, to touch their hearts and bring them to know His Son. Jesus's message reminds us that He will never leave us and that He loved us even before we loved Him. His presence and His love provide the cure for loneliness.

NOTES

1   *The Nobel Peace Prize 1979,* Mother Teresa Acceptance Speech; https://www.nobelprize.org/prizes/peace/1979/teresa/acceptance -speech/; accessed December 15, 2023.

2   "Remarks on Presenting the Presidential Medal of Freedom to Mother Teresa," *Ronald Reagan Presidential Library & Museum,* June 20, 1985; https://www.reaganlibrary.gov/archives/speech/ remarks-presenting-presidential-medal-freedom-mother-teresa; accessed December 15, 2023.

3   "Statement on Signing Legislation Conferring Honorary United States Citizenship on Mother Teresa," *The American President Project,* October 1, 1996; https://www.presidency.ucsb.edu/documents/ statement-signing-legislation-conferring-honorary-united-states -citizenship-mother-teresa; accessed December 15, 2023.

4   Kenneth J. Cooper, "Mother Teresa Dies at 87," *WashingtonPost .com,* September 6, 1997; https://www.washingtonpost.com/wp-srv/ inatl/longterm/teresa/stories/teresa0906.htm#:~:text=NEW%20 DELHI%2C%20Sept.%206%20%28Saturday%29% E6%9F%9Aother%20Teresa%2C%20the%20Nobel,%22the%20 saint%20of%20the%20gutters.%22%20She%20was%2087; accessed June 22, 2024.

5   *ITN Exclusive:* "Whatever 'in love' means" Charles and Diana Engagement Interview in Full" (1981); https://www.youtube.com/ watch?v=6lSmizRAe6A; accessed June 22, 2024. Also see *Diana: Her True Story—in Her Own Words* by Andrew Morton (New York: Simon & Schuster, 2017).

6   Simon Perry, "Jury: Driver, Paparazzi to Blame for Princess Di's Death," *People.com,* April 7, 2008; https://people.com/crime/jury

-driver-paparazzi-to-blame-for-princess-dis-death/; accessed December 15, 2023.

7 James Martin, S.J., "Remembering the unlikely friendship between Princess Diana and Mother Teresa," *America Magazine,* October 2, 1997; https://www.americamagazine.org/arts-culture/1997/10/02/remembering-unlikely-friendship-between-princess-diana-and-mother-teresa; accessed December 15, 2023.

"*Fear can paralyze us and keep us from believing God and stepping out in faith. The devil loves a fearful Christian!*"
"*Courage is contagious. When a brave man takes a stand, the spines of others are often stiffened.*"
—Reverend Billy Graham

"*For God is not the author of confusion but of peace....*"
—1 Corinthians 14:33 NKJV

"*The vague and tenuous hope that God is too kind to punish the ungodly has become a deadly opiate for the consciences of millions.*"
—A. W. Tozer

6

PROPHETIC HISTORIC EVENT 6

9/11 TERRORIST ATTACKS ON THE UNITED STATES OF AMERICA

Source: https://commons.wikimedia.org/wiki/File:Explosion_following_the
_plane_impact_into_the_South_Tower_(WTC_2)_-_B6019~11.jpg

This historic event carries with it an annual remembrance. Americans pause and remember. The media feeds us stories, shows us new data or new information, and tries to hold our attention to the reality of being attacked in our own country by people who set out to harm us.

We feel the pain, remember the horror, and reflect on the aftermath. We need to take these attacks extremely seriously. We also must pay big-time attention to what the numbers prophesy to us.

Social media feeds come on, pictures start appearing on the news, and you start hearing the rhetoric. Many of us think, *I wish we could get away from this day, but this day just keeps coming back, and it keeps coming back.*

This event is one of those defining moments in our country's life.

PROPHETIC MESSAGE

The Lord began to prepare me for this day about two years before it happened. I didn't understand it until after it happened, but it was apparent that God knew this was on the calendar and that this moment would be important to the United States and to the American people in a personal and critical way.

I received a word from the Lord about two years before that there was going to be a big revival when a certain big event took place. I knew it had to do with buildings falling down. There were many details in the vision I had, and I'm not going to cover all of it here. God Almighty gave me a powerful dream to begin to speak His word to me. In it, I was going down a staircase, and the building fell while I was in it.

After the rubble cleared and after the dust finally settled, I could see all the churches in America, and they were all on fire. As soon as I saw the buildings come down on 9/11, I knew this was what the Lord was talking to me about. I knew there was about to be a revival.

I don't know if you remember the national revival that took place immediately following 9/11, but there was a great move among the people of God to humble themselves. It was strong, and people knew being part of what God was about was what was real. There were so many who wanted to be part of that.

Our country saw our friends in New York covered with ashes. Throughout the Bible, being covered in ashes has to do with mourning. When we saw those people coming out of the smoke covered in ashes, we all mourned because of the scene before our eyes.

Source: Halasy, Don, photographer. Man covered with ashes assisting a woman walking and holding a particle mask to her face, following the September 11th terrorist attack on the World Trade Center, New York City / Don Halasy. New York, ca. 2001. Photograph. https://www.loc.gov/item/2002716964/.

Because He wants His people to know and understand what He is saying, He started giving me a message for the church well before any of this actually happened. I was preaching a series called 9/11, which I began three weeks before the attack. Because it takes time to prepare a sermon series, He had been talking to me incessantly about 9 and 11 for weeks before. I couldn't get away from 9 and 11; everywhere I looked, I saw 9 and 11. I heard God speak, but I didn't have a clue what He was saying. I just couldn't get away from the numbers 9 and 11.

What's interesting is that we don't call this event September 11th; we call it 9/11 because the prophetic values of the numbers are the message. The 9 and the 11 are the message that God Almighty wants us to hear. Have you ever thought about that? We don't call it September 11th. We call it 9/11.

Source: https://catalog.archives.gov/id/6527847

I was actually preaching through the 9/11 Scriptures at the time. I kept saying to Leanna and others around me, "Is anybody else seeing 9/11 besides me?" I know that might sound strange or weird to you, but when you realize the importance of God's message through numbers, that's kind of normal speech. You start seeing a pattern, or you start seeing some kind of a prophetic pattern, so you know that it's the Lord; but just because God is speaking and you know it's Him doesn't mean you understand it.

You have to search out the matter. I was actually searching out the matter. I didn't get on a bullhorn and announce to the world that something terrible was going to happen in New York. I was preaching on 9/11 before and during the 9/11 event.

God considered this an important event and wanted to give me a head start, so I was prepared to bring a message to the church at a time when they needed to be encouraged about what He was saying.

THE NUMBERS THAT PROPHESY
WHAT THE NUMBERS ARE SAYING TO US.

9 In the positive represents fruit-bearing. Nine months to carry a baby to term. Nine fruits listed in the fruit of the Spirit in Galatians.

9 In the negative represents judgment. Particularly judgment upon disorder if we won't let God be God.

11 In the positive represents heroes rising up.

11 In the negative represents disorder.

As we consider this negative event, we clearly get the message that it was a judgment on disorder. God is saying, "This is what happens when you don't let Me be Me."

Judgment is out there 24 hours a day, 7 days a week, trying to get you to feel condemned or defeated. Yet God says, "No, this one is Mine." As soon as you step out from under the dome of God Almighty, you step into a place of judgment, and that's on you. It's not because of anybody else. It's not on God.

God is not mean. He's not waiting for us to make Him angry so He can judge us. God sent His Son to the world as a sacrifice for our sins. When we receive Jesus as our Savior, we step out of the judgment we deserve because of our sins. Jesus's blood proclaims we are redeemed and no longer have to pay for our sins.

We need to understand how judgment works. The book of Revelation describes a time when God Almighty listens to the voice of the martyrs crying out, saying, "How much longer must we wait until our murders have been avenged?" The prayers of the saints are no longer there.

It is interesting that before the 9/11 tragedy, the United States set up the phone number 911 to call in case of an emergency. If a medical or police emergency, we dialed 911 then as we do now.

New York is famous for many things. One area that has an international focus is Wall Street, which is represented by the iconic charging bull. The statue has a golden look to it, almost like the golden calf. On the day the World Trade Center towers fell, the attention of New York changed from the bull in front of Wall Street to Church Street. That is the street the towers fell on as the whole world watched.

Nine represents judgment, and 11 represents disorder. God is simply saying, this is the judgment that happens when I'm not God ruling in your life. Here's the good news: you don't have to stay in a realm of judgment. You have a choice, and you can move over into Redemption.

Sin brings judgment upon us. What do we need to do? We need to repent, which means turning away from sin and turning to God to ask Him to rule in our lives.

There are different signs reflecting repentance. One word for repentance is weeping, and an Old Testament sign is to wear sackcloth, which is like a burlap sack. Sackcloth is uncomfortable and rough.

As we discuss these words, let's consider their gematria. Remember, this their numeric value.

- *Sin* has a numerical value of 911. *Weep* has a numerical value of 911, and the word *sackcloth* has a numerical value of 911.

- There are so many messages about this, we can't miss the voice in the thunder. God wants us to see the number 11.

- New York is known as the Empire State. As a type and shadow, an empire is in direct opposition to a kingdom.

- The day of the attack was 9-11. Nine plus 1 plus 1 equals 11.

- September 11 is the 254th day of the year. Two plus 5 plus 4 equals 11.

- After September 11, there are exactly 111 days left until the end of the year.

- Henry Hudson discovered Manhattan Island on September 11, 1609.

- New York is the 11th state in the Union.

- The first plane to hit the tower was Flight 11.

- Flight 11 had 92 people on board. Nine plus 2 equals 11.

- Flight 11 had 11 crew members—2 pilots and 9 flight attendants.

- Flight 77 had 65 passengers on board—6 plus 5 equals 11.

- The twin towers standing together look like an 11.

- Both World Trade Center towers had 110 stories; that's an 11 with zero behind it.

- The North Tower, the first World Trade Center tower hit, collapsed at 10:28 a.m. One plus 2 plus 8 equals 11.

- The World Trade Center towers collapsed to a height of 11 stories.

- The rubble was 11 stories tall.

- FDNY Unit 1 was the first fire unit to arrive at the World Trade Center towers, and 11 firefighters perished.

- New York City has 11 letters.

- Afghanistan has 11 letters.

- The Pentagon has 11 letters.

- Henry Hudson has 11 letters.

The World Trade Center's fires burned continuously for 99 days from September 11 to December 19, 2001, and it is the longest-burning commercial fire in all of US history.

On September 7, 2002, the New York Medical Examiner announced the revised official death toll for the World Trade Center attacks was 2,801 human beings who woke up that morning, ate their breakfast, and had the audacity to actually go to work the morning of September 11, 2001.

One year to the date later, the names of 2,801 victims were read at a Ground Zero ceremony; it took two and a half hours to read all the names.

Exactly one year after the disaster, something else incredible happened that caused many to start talking about the numbers 9 and 11. On September 11, 2002, New Yorkers thought someone was playing a cruel joke when Fox News announced that the New York Lottery drew 911 as the winning Pick Three on 9/11.

That is astonishing. Our God is an astonishing God who wants to talk to us in many ways. This event is covered in 9 11 judgment of the disorder that is in our country. We were in the wrong place, leaving God out of everything. We need to be in the right place. God wants to see us in a position of restoration, which requires us to turn to Him.

PROMISES

I want to give you some promises from God that are 9/11 on the positive side.

When we are faced with something incredibly serious or painful, what do we do? What do we need to know?

We need to know who God is to us and who we are to God. We also need to know how to stand up on His word and trust Him.

The very first covenant Scripture in the Bible, a promise from Him that is never going to change, is Genesis 9:11!

> *Thus I establish My covenant with you: Never again shall all flesh be cut off by the waters of the flood; never again shall there be a flood to destroy the earth.*

Nothing can stand up against the power of God. He will come against them to prevent it. Here we see boils were used to stop them in Exodus 9:11 (NKJV):

And the magicians could not stand before Moses because of the boils, for the boils were on the magicians and on all the Egyptians.

But my favorite is Amos 9:11. Amos 911 is a prophetic marker that addresses the end days:

On that day, I will raise up the Tabernacle of David, which has fallen down, and repair its damages; I will raise up its ruins, and rebuild it as in the days of old...."

Many Scriptures indicate the third temple will be built, yet also indicate that the antichrist will rule it. I'm not saying that's not going to happen where the Dome of the Rock is now. But God's desire is not to rebuild a temple with a certain order that allows only one person to get into God's presence. That is the temple of Solomon that was built after the Tabernacle of Moses, who brought the law.

I'm looking at the third temple as I look at His followers. I think the third temple Jesus is rebuilding is us.

God's desire is to rebuild David's tabernacle. That was where David brought in the Ark of the Covenant, which represented the presence of God. David put a tent over the top, but it had no walls so that everyone had access to it 24 hours, 7 days a week. It didn't matter who you were; all you had to do was come into the presence and worship.

David inquired before the Lord, and he cried out to God in broad daylight. He fell to the floor and bowed his face and cried out because he wanted to be in the presence of the Lord. His heart was that if he got into the Lord's presence, he would take everybody else with him. God's desire for the last days is in the midst of the ruins. He's building His Kingdom and giving everyone access to His presence, access to His word, and access to His glory.

SCRIPTURES THAT CONFIRM

On that day I will raise up the tabernacle of David, which has fallen down, and repair its damages; I will raise up its ruins, and rebuild it as in the days of old (Amos 9:11 NKJV).

Thus I establish My covenant with you: Never again shall all flesh be cut off by the waters of the flood; never again shall there be a flood to destroy the earth (Genesis 9:11 NKJV).

And the magicians could not stand before Moses because of the boils, for the boils were on the magicians and on all the Egyptians (Exodus 9:11 NKJV).

And it came to pass, at the end of forty days and forty nights, that the Lord gave me the two tablets of stone, the tablets of the covenant (Deuteronomy 9:11 NKJV).

Then Ziba said to the king, "According to all that my lord the king has commanded his servant, so will your servant do." "As for Mephibosheth," said the king, "he shall eat at my table like one of the king's sons" (2 Samuel 9:11 NKJV).

Then Jehu came out to the servants of his master, and one said to him, "Is all well? Why did this madman come to you?" And he said to them, "You know the man and his babble" (2 Kings 9:11 NKJV).

On that day the number of those who were killed in Shushan the citadel was brought to the king (Esther 9:11 NKJV).

I returned and saw under the sun that—the race is not to the swift, nor the battle to the strong, nor bread to the wise, nor riches to men of understanding, nor favor to men of skill; but time and chance happen to them all (Ecclesiastes 9:11 NKJV).

Yes, all Israel has transgressed Your law, and has departed so as not to obey Your voice; therefore the curse and the oath written in the Law of Moses the servant of God have been poured out on us, because we have sinned against Him (Daniel 9:11 NKJV).

Therefore the Lord shall set up the adversaries of Rezin against him, and spur his enemies on (Isaiah 9:11 NKJV).

I will make Jerusalem a heap of ruins, a den of jackals. I will make the cities of Judah desolate, without an inhabitant (Jeremiah 9:11 NKJV).

And when the Pharisees saw it, they said to His disciples, "Why does your Teacher eat with tax collectors and sinners?" (Matthew 9:11 NKJV)

And they had as king over them the angel of the bottomless pit, whose name in Hebrew is Abaddon, but in Greek he has the name Apollyon (Revelation 9:11 NKJV).

SUMMARY FACTS

LAST THOUGHTS

The memorial of the Lord that stands forever, *"the solid foundation of God stands, having this seal: 'The Lord knew those who are His,' and, 'Let everyone who names the name of Christ depart from iniquity'"* (2 Timothy 2:19 NKJV).

None of us will forget the terrible attacks on 9/11. Focusing on the message we have heard so clearly from the Lord, I hope you will let it be a different memorial.

The foundation of God stands sure. He knows who are His, but we must heed this message from Him. There is available to us the ability to be heroes of the faith, rising up to produce fruit in the Kingdom and bring Him glory.

His message from that day in 2001 tells us emphatically there will be judgment that will bring calamity into our lives if we persist in living in disorder and keeping God out of our lives.

It's up to us, but this message from Him assures that we can turn 9/11 into a memorial that reminds us that we need God and desire His redemption and the peaceful, fruit-bearing life of order that He gives us.

LEAP OF FAITH*

When the sun finally came up, it proved to be a beautiful Tuesday morning. Cool fall air and not a cloud in the sky made the morning commute to downtown Manhattan seem a little more pleasant than usual. Jonathan Briley walked into the World Trade Center that fateful day, looking up, as always. I think about him.

The son of a Baptist pastor, Jonathan grew up working on his daddy's PA system. His interest in music and speaking eventually landed him a job as the sound engineer at the famed restaurant Windows of the World. Anytime there was a conference or a celebration, it was Jonathan's job to set up and run the sound equipment.

On September 11, 2001, the restaurant was holding a breakfast for 16 members of the Waters Financial Technology Congress and 71 other guests. It was a day Jonathan had to be there early. About 20 minutes after he arrived, American Airlines Flight 11 slammed into the North Tower just a few stories beneath him.

Eating in that same restaurant was Alayne Gentul, 44, a senior vice president of the Fiduciary Trust and mother of two. As the room began to fill up with smoke, she called her husband.

"Smoke is coming in from everywhere, Jack," she labored to tell her husband. Guys are breaking the windows."

"Honey, go to the stairs and get out of there."

"We can't," she responded, "it's too hot in the stairs. Like an oven."

So many terrible things happened that day we will not forget. Some, we will want to. As the estimated 1,000 people trapped on floors 100 through 107 began trying to move away from the inferno, New Yorkers looked up with their hands over their mouths.

A photojournalist named Richard Drew lived close to the towers. Richard was already no stranger to history. He had been one of only four photographers in the room when Bobby Kennedy was assassinated nearly 40 years earlier.

At 9:41 am, 56 minutes after the ordeal had started, Richard pointed his lens upward and caught a man falling. He took 12 pictures of Jonathan Briley as he plunged 1,300 feet to Church Street below. It's believed that Jonathan is the famous "falling man." The picture seen by millions throughout the world of a person headed straight down, completely vertical, almost casual.

His arms are by his side; his left leg is bent at the knee, and his white jacket billowing free against black pants. In the one famous picture, he perfectly splits the towers. The north tower is to his left and the south tower to his right. It is an amazing photograph and one most of us wish we hadn't seen.

Jonathan was asthmatic, and the toxic fumes forced him outside for almost an hour before he took flight. I think he thought it better to die flying than to die choking. In a place where every option had been taken away from him, he somehow mustered the courage to step out of the heat and into the hands of God.

In one of many interviews, Jonathan's elder sister, Gwendolyn, says: "When I first looked at the picture...and I saw it was a man like him, tall and slim, I said, 'If I didn't know any better, that could be Jonathan.'"

When asked if his apparent jumping collided with their Christian theology, she said something I think is quite brilliant. "Let me tell you how much Jonathan loved God. He trusted Him so much that he jumped 105 stories expecting God to catch him." To Gwendolyn there was victory for her brother even in this tragedy...especially in this tragedy.

No matter what terrible thing we are facing today, it pales compared to what Jonathan faced. Whatever tough decisions, I hope we have the courage to trust God when nothing else makes sense. Jonathan Briley and his sister Gwendolyn preach to me. They help me. I believe the next time we see Jonathan; he won't be falling at all...he'll be risen. Now that's a picture I want to see.

*From my book *Best of the Brewer*

"So when this corruptible has put on incorruption, and this mortal has put on immortality, then shall be brought to pass the saying that is written: "Death is swallowed up in victory"
(1 Corinthians 15:54 NKJV).

To hear God speak, to have His voice go through and through the soul, involves a great responsibility, yet he who truly feels it will never wish to shirk it.
—Charles Hadden Spurgeon

"In my opinion, the greatest sin in the church of Jesus Christ in this generation is ignorance of the Word of God."
—J. Vernon McGee

"The Lord your God will raise up for you a prophet like me from among you, from your fellow Israelites. You must listen to him."
—Moses, Deuteronomy 18:15 NIV

7

THE HYPE OF TYPE

A SYNOPSIS OF WAYS GOD SPEAKS

NUMBERS   SHADOWS

EARTHQUAKES

TYPES   DREAMS

WONDERS

WIND

VISIONS   THUNDER

STILL SMALL VOICE

The word *typology* means studying all the ways God speaks through types, shadows, symbols, numbers, and secrets. To understand types and shadows, we have to look at the heavenly language of symbols and parables. However, to understand symbols and parables, we first need to understand how God speaks and why we should dedicate our lives to pursuing His word and following His heart.

I never go searching for ways to minister. God knows what I am to do, so He brings me a ministry that He knows I will do well with. He brought me deeply into a place of study and searching out the ways He speaks to us.

God is speaking to you right now, and it is a word that changes everything. It is a word that is in direct contrast to what the world is saying. He brings a word that will give you a different focus and a different lens so you can see something that you *must* see because it is a message from God Himself. As His people, we must be people who hear God speak. To understand His voice today, we must remember what He has said in the past.

THE GHOST OF CHRISTMAS PAST

In Dickens's timeless story, the ghost of Christmas past comes to Ebenezer Scrooge when he is sleeping to say, "Rise and walk with me!" The scenes that follow represent looking at memories from the past to remember their importance.

We have the Holy Ghost sent to live in us for a similar yet greater purpose:

> *But the Helper, the Holy Spirit, whom the Father will send in My name, He will teach you all things, and bring to your remembrance all things that I said to you* (John 14:26 NKJV).

The word *remember* is found in the Bible 631 times. God remembers His people, His covenant, and His promises. Throughout the

Scriptures, His people are told to remember, too. The root of the word means to be mindful of or concerned about.

> *Remember the former things of old, for I am God, and there is no other; I am God, and there is none like Me, declaring the end from the beginning, and from ancient times, things that are not yet done...* (Isaiah 46:9-10 NKJV).

If we are "asleep" prophetically, we will miss the profound revelations God has shown us in the past and the transformative insights He is showing us today. We must rise and walk with the Lord, fully aware of what He has done, what He is doing, and what He has yet to do.

An important day in Jewish history is the 9th of Av, which is the 9th day of the 11th month on the Hebrew calendar. That was the day when the 10 spies gave a bad report about God's Promised Land. They doubted God, even though they had seen miracles, signs, and wonders from the Lord in their past. Since then, there had been a repeat of disasters on that day throughout their history.

God addressed the people's rebellion and reminded them He had been faithful as their covenantal God. He spoke to His people on their 9 11 back then and has continued to speak in disasters to warn them since then. He also spoke through disaster to America on 9/11 because we have not honored Him.

The voice of God is saying, "Remember what has happened. Repent from your rebellion. Remember the good I have done in your past. Remember My promises that I made for those who let Me be their God. Let it give you hope for the future things I want to do. Let it help you listen to My voice in the world around you today."

PROPHETIC PREMISES

There are 3 premises we are going to consider. A premise is a proposition that leads you to a conclusion. As we develop our prophetic skill sets, we need to understand these 3 things:

- **Premise 1** – God is speaking clearly to all of us right now—and every Christian can and must hear God speak prophetically.

- **Premise 2** – God is not limited to certain voices that carry His word or the means of delivery for His word. We must allow God to speak in any arena He chooses.

- **Premise 3** – Within every word God gives to His church corporately, there is a word for us as a part of the body of the church and for each of us individually.

Let's look at each premise more closely.

PREMISE 1

God is speaking clearly to all of us right now—and every Christian can and must hear God speak prophetically.

Everything prophetic has an offensive nature to it. That is why many in the church don't want to have anything to do with it. They can't get past the offense. They say it is unsafe; there is no formula you can apply. Also, since God is unlimited, He can speak through things you don't believe He would speak through. Just because God is speaking through something, however, doesn't mean He is in agreement with what He is speaking through.

To understand this better, we can look at Matthew 16:17-18 (NKJV):

Jesus answered and said to him, "Blessed are you, Simon Bar-Jonah, for flesh and blood has not revealed this to you, but My Father who is in heaven. And I also say to you that you are Peter, and on this rock, I will build My church, and the gates of Hades shall not prevail against it."

Jesus took the 12 disciples to Caesarea Philippi, an offensive place. The name of the place, when seen through our prophetic lens, speaks of many things we will miss if we don't open our eyes to see. Jesus took them to that place to say to them, "Who do *you* say that I am?" (see Matthew 16:13-16 NKJV).

This place was named after Caesar because it was a place created for worshipping him. It is the den of satan, a very offensive place. Caesar means "I am god." It was built and named by King Herod, Philip the Second. He was the son of Herod the Great and a descendant of Cleopatra. He was a dictator in that region, and he was supposed to govern for the benefit of the Jews. He wasn't a Jew, however; in fact, he hated the Jews. He instead worked for the benefit of Rome. He built this as a pagan place to worship Caesar, and then he stuck his name on it.

Imagine if Muslims came to our country and built a temple to worship Saddam Hussein. Then imagine Jesus taking us there for an excursion one day. It is in that context where we find this teaching from Him. He was using the types and shadows of that place to say that the world is saying *this* is how all of life is supposed to be. The world is saying that you should place your trust here and worship these things.

In this story, we find God going to the temple of a guy who calls himself "god." We see the King of the Jews going to a place that was built by a man who was supposed to be the king of the Jews. In that demonic place, He asked His disciples to tell Him what the world was saying about who He was. Then He asks the most important question, "Who do you say I am?"

Peter says he knows exactly who Jesus is, *"You are the Messiah, the Son of the living God."*

Jesus turned and said, "Simon, son of Jonah," The name Simon actually means "shifty," so He is saying that Simon is not very solid. Then Jesus points out that Simon comes from the bloodline of Jonah. In effect, He's saying, "This revelation doesn't come from you or your bloodline, Simon. My Father has personally spoken to you. He has interrupted your physical bloodline and your timeline and has personally spoken this to you. So, now I will change your name to Peter."

In that moment of divine revelation, Jesus knew His disciple had moved from shifty to rock solid. *It is upon this rock I will build my church, and the gates of hell will not prevail against it.*

Friend, this is fundamental Christianity 101; this truth is basic to our faith.

No one is a Christian unless they hear the Father speak.

There is no such thing as Christianity outside of the personal revelation that comes through Jesus from the Father. You become a prophetic person when the Father reveals His heart to you.

There is confirmation for us when we search out a verse that is familiar to us, *"So then faith comes by hearing, and hearing by the word of God"* (Romans 10:17 NKJV).

Going to Strong's Concordance, we find the Greek word translated *word* in Romans 10:17 is #4487, rhēma, which means a spoken word, made "by the living voice." It is commonly used in the New Testament for the Lord speaking His dynamic, living word in a believer to inbirth faith ("His inwrought persuasion").

Faith comes by hearing God's supernatural word. The church is built upon the revelation that God speaks to His children. This is the rock the church is built on. If you have faith in the Lord Jesus Christ, you have heard God. When you hear and obey God, He can use you to build His church and expand His Kingdom on earth.

Scriptures repeatedly tell all who will listen that God is speaking to us. It is, in fact, a very foundational principle.

- Hebrews 6:1 NKJV – (The peril of Not Progressing) *Therefore, leaving the discussion of the elementary principles of Christ, let us go on to perfection, not laying again the foundation of repentance from dead works and of faith toward God.*

- Jeremiah 33:3 NKJV – *Call to Me and I will answer you, and will show you great and mighty things, which you do not know.*

- Amos 3:7-8 KJV – *Surely the Lord God will do nothing, but he revealeth his secret unto his servants the prophets. The lion hath roared, who will not fear? the Lord God hath spoken, who can but prophesy?*

- Numbers 11:29 KJV – *...would God that all the Lord's people were prophets....*

- 1 Corinthians 14:1,31,39 NKJV – *Pursue love, and desire spiritual gifts, but especially that you may prophesy. ...For you can all prophesy one by one, that all may learn and all may be encouraged. ...Therefore, brethren, desire earnestly to prophesy, and do not forbid to speak with tongues.*

- Isaiah 30:21 NKJV – *Your ears shall hear a word behind you, saying, "This is the way, walk in it," whenever you turn to the right hand or when you turn to the left.*

When we have God inside us, He sends us forth and moves behind us. He will show us where and how to move, but He wants us to do what He shows us.

- Mark 4:24 ESV – *And he said to them, "Pay attention to what you hear: with the measure you use, it will be measured to you, and still more will be added to you."*

The more committed we are to listening for God and obeying what He tells us, the more He will talk to us.

- Luke 11:28 ESV – *But he said, "Blessed rather are those who hear the word of God and keep it!"*
- John 10:27 ESV – *My sheep hear my voice, and I know them, and they follow me.*

We should never hesitate to tell our Christian friends that we have heard God. I don't know how you hear God, but I do know that God is not limited in the ways He speaks to His children.

The power to possess breakthrough comes from hearing the word of God. The church whose foundation is built on personal revelation of Jesus Christ by the mouth of God Himself is the church with the power to break through obstacles.

But Jesus replied, "It is written and forever remains written,
'Man shall not live by bread alone, but by every word that
comes out of the mouth of God'" (Matthew 4:4 AMP).

Your ability to get past all the enemy's barriers, the gates of hell, is directly tied to your ability to hear God speak.

If you have come up against a new wall or a new barrier, then you need a new word. You need to hear what God has to say to you so you can overcome whatever it is. You need a new level of renewed faith that comes from a fresh word from God.

On this rock, I will build my church, and the gates of hell will
not prevail.

That verse from Matthew 16:18 doesn't just mean that the church is invading hell; it means that Heaven is invading Earth. Hearing God speak and obeying what He says gives you the power and authority to break through. Breaking down the gates of hell comes from experiencing personal, intimate revelations from God.

The following are five monster reasons why hearing the voice of God is so offensive to the church and how we can overcome those reasons. Confronting these is important so we can have wisdom in this area.

Monster Reason 1: Just because God is speaking does not mean you know it.

You have to be a seeker to hear His voice. *"For God speaketh once, yea twice, yet man perceiveth it not"* (Job 33:14 KJV).

He is speaking all the time; but we just don't know it. If He were speaking, would you know it?

Psalm 18:13 (NKJV) says, "*The Lord thundered from heaven, and the Most High uttered His voice; hailstones and coals of fire.*"

We think, yes, of course, I would know that was God. But what if He spoke in a still, small voice?

And behold, the Lord passed by, and a great and strong wind tore into the mountains and broke the rocks in pieces before the Lord, but the Lord was not in the wind; and after the wind an earthquake, but the Lord was not in the earthquake; and after the earthquake a fire, but the Lord was not in the fire; and after the fire a still small voice.

So it was, when Elijah heard it, that he wrapped his face in his mantle and went out and stood in the entrance of the cave (1 Kings 19:11-13 NKJV).

Elijah wasn't moved by the wind, the earthquake, or the fire, but when God spoke to him in His still, small voice, Elijah was overcome and moved toward God. Sometimes, He speaks in a whisper, and sometimes He speaks at the volume of thunder, but He is heard because of a still and quiet heart listening for Him.

Monster Reason 2: Just because you know He is speaking doesn't mean you always understand it.

You have to be willing to search out the matter.

Proverbs 25:2 NKJV – *It is the glory of God to conceal a matter, but the glory of kings is to search out a matter.*

Psalm 78:2 NKJV – *I will open my mouth in a parable; I will utter dark sayings of old.*

You only qualify for hearing Him speak if you love Him. Some only hear the thunder and think parables are only interesting stories. When we love Him, we hear and understand the mysteries.

Romans 1:20 NKJV – *For since the creation of the world, His invisible attributes are clearly seen, being understood by the things that are made, even His eternal power and Godhead, so that they are without excuse.*

God is speaking and revealing amazing things around us all the time. We must be aware and listen. God sees your life, He knows what affects you, and He hides His word within that. Those who want a relationship with Him, notice and look into those things.

Therefore I speak to them in parables, because seeing they do not see, and hearing they do not hear, nor do they understand (Matthew 13:13 NKJV).

1. God speaks to us in parables.

Matthew 13:13 is a Scripture we need to understand because it explains why He speaks in parables. He is saying, "I don't want them to get it. This word is not for everybody because not everybody is eligible. You have to love Me to get it. I'm not going to give you My heart if you aren't going to be a man after my heart." In the International Children's Bible, this verse reads, "This is why I use stories to teach the people: They see, but they don't really see. They hear, but they don't really understand."

2. Rebellion demands the benefits of the Kingdom without wanting the King.

Thirteen is the number of rebellion, and Genesis 13:13 (NKJV) describes what spiritual rebellion is: *"But the men of Sodom were exceedingly wicked and sinful against the Lord."*

Rebellion demands the benefits of the Kingdom without wanting the King. It is loving the things God offers you without loving God. Rebellion is when you self-identify instead of conforming yourself to God's true identity of who you are.

3. You must be willing to be committed and consecrated to a life of contemplation.

God uses parables and symbols, types and shadows, pictures, allegories, and prophetic pieces that must be charted out, one piece at a time. You must be willing to be committed and consecrated to a life of contemplation. Don't let the word of God depart from your head 24/7!

PREMISE 2

God is not limited to certain voices that carry His word or the means of delivery for His word. We must allow God to speak in any arena He chooses.

> Psalm 29:3 NKJV – *The voice of the Lord is over the waters; the God of glory thunders; the Lord is over many waters.*

In Revelation 14:2 (NKJV), John relates how he heard God: *"And I heard a voice from heaven, like the voice of many waters, and like the voice of loud thunder. And I heard the sound of harpists playing their harps."*

John was a diligent listener. He heard God in the wind, the numbers, the Scriptures, through everything. God wasn't speaking in only one way then. His message to us will also come in many ways now because He wants us to hear Him.

We must develop this skill set. If you don't think you have this ability, seek Him for the ability. God wants you to want to hear Him badly enough that you will hunger to hear Him. He wants us to dig deep to find what He is saying because it shows Him how much we desire a relationship with Him.

> Hebrews 5:13-14 NKJV – *For everyone who partakes only of milk is unskilled in the word of righteousness, for he is a babe. But solid food belongs to those who are of full age, that is, those who by reason of use have their senses exercised to discern both good and evil.*

This Scripture passage tells us it takes practice to mature as a Christian. We must exercise our senses. As we practice hearing Him, we will learn discernment so we will know what is of God and what isn't.

Monster Reason 3: Just because you understand it, doesn't mean you know what to do with it. It doesn't mean you know how to deliver it.

You have to demonstrate how Jesus would say it. You have to know Jesus to know what to deliver and how to deliver it.

Monster Reason 4: Just because you know what to do with it, doesn't mean that you know what the outcome will be.

Kingdom is all about relationships. Everything about the Kingdom is first relational before it is functional. So, there is often a lot of fruit before success. God is more about fruit than He is about success.

Monster Reason 5: Just because you know what the outcome will be doesn't mean it will automatically happen.

As the parable of the seeker tells us, there are always varying degrees of harvest: some will be 30 times greater, some will be 60 times greater, and some will be 100 times greater. We must become people who love the process and the journey instead of just wanting the ending.

That's what warlocks do. They don't want to know God. They don't want anything to do with the process; they just want to do the hokey pokey, turn themselves around, and boom, they have power.

Believers on the other hand have to walk it out to the end. God will see that you are paying attention to what He is saying, and He will give you a new measure of hearing from Him.

There is tremendous prophetic value in the headlines of current events. There are types in our culture found in the lives and in the situations that make headlines. Learning to pay attention to those and asking God to reveal what He is saying is important for us all. We are not all called into the office of prophecy, but we are all given the gift of prophecy.

Years ago, I was deeply impressed by the teaching from Rick Joyner's book *The Harvest,* when he wrote:

To interpret current events in the light of Divine Purpose is the primary function of the prophets. They must see the relationships of events in conjunction with God's works. And His Word. Prophetic people do not just foretell or predict. Much of the ministry of prophecy is devoted to the explanation of current signs and messages. There are extraordinary events happening today that do have a message for those that have an ear to hear.[1]

My true interest in searching out the prophetic began while I was sitting on the back porch with my Papa. We were sitting out there, not talking, just watching the sun go down. The glow of the sun as it set was matching the red-orange glow of the pipe my Papa was smoking. This is one of my favorite memories. I was mesmerized by his pipe. There are times when I am in the profound presence of the Lord when I can smell Papa's pipe. After a few moments, he took his pipe out of his mouth and used the stem end of it to point. "Hoss," he said, "do you see that tree out there?" I said, "Yes, sir."

He said, "That tree is the last one to lose its leaves every fall, and it is the first one to get new leaves in the springtime. I think God may be saying something to me about that." He then put his pipe back in his mouth.

I instantly and prophetically knew what the Lord was saying to my Papa. I said, "Papa, that's exactly what the Bible says. 'The last shall be first, and the first shall be last.'"

He looked back over at me and smiled. Then he turned back to his Bible and said, "Look." One of his favorite preachers had sent out a monthly message that was next to his Bible. It said that Scripture on its headlines: "The last shall be first, and the first shall be last." Then my Papa said, "Well, looky there, the Lord is preaching through that tree right over there."

Right there, as Heaven was invading this Earth that I was on, I began to be aware that, "Oh my, God is speaking!" I began to suspect that He was speaking a lot louder and a lot more than I ever realized. It was an incredible moment when everything started to change for me, and it began with my grandfather.

From then on, as I studied the Bible, I would compare what it said to events of the day. When I saw headlines, I would ask, "If this were a dream, what would it mean?" As I was driving, I would look at the license plates in front of me and ask questions such as, "If I dreamed there was a bright red Corvette in front of me with the license plate *Jezebel*, would that be a word from the Lord that I needed to change lanes somehow?" That's a true story, and when it happened, my response was, "I don't know what You're saying, but I'm not staying in this lane!"

I began thinking that maybe the word of God is in all of creation somehow. God began to show me how He used things all around us to speak to us. John the Baptist said that he was "The voice of one crying in the wilderness." There are many voices sharing God's messages. There are events that have the voice of the Lord. There are things that contain the voice of the Lord.

Remember, "The voice of the Lord is over the waters." What happens when you speak when you are on the water? Your voice is amplified. God is speaking in many ways because He doesn't want us to miss what He is saying to us. Current events that get our attention are one of the ways God gets our attention.

We think pop culture can't bring a message from God because He isn't part of what is going on in that situation. But that is a wrong thought. We need to ask what God is saying to us in that evil. He always answers evil with goodness. If we don't hear Him and search Him out in evil, we will miss what He wants to say to us to teach us about His Good.

Let's look a bit deeper into the Bible's example of God speaking His word through pop culture that was evil. It was briefly mentioned in the beginning of this book. Looking deeply reveals other elements. In the Roman culture in those days, they set up locations designed to be party centers. They built the infrastructure to make it easy to get there, included lots of fun things to do, and made them attractive to people. Pompei was an example of one of those places. Laodicea was another that was very special. Several miles north of it, there were hot springs.

The people decided they would develop a way to bring that hot water down and provide the homes with running hot water. The world had never seen hot water in homes before. Then someone realized there were also springs several miles to the south that had springs coming from deep in the ground with super cold, good water. The idea was developed, and they built an elaborate open-air aqueduct system bringing water from the north and from the south. This gave them houses with hot and cold running water. There was great excitement about this development.

There was a general who came to the "ribbon cutting ceremony" to launch this great advancement. He was known for his brutality; he would kill you if you crossed him, and everyone feared him. In an effort to make him more likable, the people began to get him involved in events that would soften his image with the people.

On the day of the great presentation of this new concept, he showed up to be the one to announce to the world that Laodicea was a place that had its act together and had something wonderful that no one else could offer the people. He took a sip from the cupful of water that he dipped out of the hot water. Then, he took a sip from the cold water. He was supposed to then proclaim how wonderful this all was.

Instead, the general spit it out! As the water traveled miles in the aqueduct, it became air temperature. He announced it was not as they had promised because instead of hot and cold running water, they had lukewarm water. He expounded on the fact that no one liked luke-warm water, adding that he ought to kill somebody over this! Instead of becoming famous for their great accomplishments, Laodicea was shamed, and they never recovered from this.

In Revelation 3:14-16 (NKJV), Jesus says, *"And to the angel of the church of the Laodiceans write, 'These things says the Amen, the Faithful and True Witness, the Beginning of the creation of God: "I know your works, that you are neither cold nor hot. I could wish you were cold or hot. So then, because you are lukewarm and neither cold nor hot, I will vomit you out of My mouth."'"*

This is Jesus speaking to a church from the headlines, and they knew the language. This was the headline in that day; today it would be the equivalent of *People* magazine or *Vanity Fair* or *Time* magazine. Jesus Christ used the headlines to bring the word of God to the people of that region in a language they could understand.

PREMISE 3

Within every word God gives to His church corporately, there is a word for us as a part of the body of the church and for each of us individually.

God spoke to the church 2,000 years ago using their culture. He is speaking to us today from the message He gave them. He is also still speaking through today's headlines from the events in our culture. God is not at all intimidated by ungodly systems. His story is in all the constellations and people worship that. In the wilderness, He was lifted up as a serpent on a pole and that is what the Egyptians worshipped and received healing. When they saw the serpent on the pole, they were healed by God. Why? Because they thought they would be healed if they put a serpent on a pole, lifted it up, and looked at it. He used their pop culture beliefs to show them His power.

He used the prophet Jeremiah in a one-one-one Scripture to speak to us. One repeated 3 times is the numerical number of Jehovah, which means God is right here right now, and we are in unity.

> Jeremiah 1:11-14 NKJV – *Moreover the word of the Lord came to me, saying, "Jeremiah, what do you see?" And I said, "I see a branch of an almond tree." Then the Lord said to me, "You have seen well, for I am ready to perform My word." And the word of the Lord came to me the second time, saying, "What do you see?" And I said, "I see a boiling pot, and it is facing away from the north." Then the Lord said to me: "Out of the north calamity shall break forth on all the inhabitants of the land."*

> Verse 11: *Moreover the word of the Lord came to me, saying, "Jeremiah, what do you see?"*

God is saying, look at what is in front of you, tell me what you see, and then I can tell you my word that is coming through that: *"And I said, 'I see a branch of an almond tree.'"*

Verse 12: *Then the Lord said to me, "You have seen well, for I am ready to perform My word."*

You have to search this out. When you do, you find that in Hebrew, the word for *almond tree* is the exact same word as *accelerate*. God confirms that His message is in what Jeremiah is seeing. He is saying He is accelerating what He has told the people He will do.

Verse 13: *And the word of the Lord came to me the second time, saying, "What do you see?" And I said, "I see a boiling pot, and it is facing away from the north."*

As this continues, Jeremiah begins to really look for the details. Not only does he see the pot, he notices its position. This brings a greater revelation from the Lord.

Verse 14: *Then the Lord said to me: "Out of the north calamity shall break forth on all the inhabitants of the land."*

When you notice the details in ordinary things around you, God can give you a powerful word. He was telling Jeremiah there was an army coming from the north and the south, and he needed to tell Israel to get out of there. That is how God speaks prophetically.

Because of man's rebellion, God puts His word in the ordinary things all around us to help us hear Him. He wants us to hear Him, and He makes sure we don't have an excuse for not hearing Him. No one can stand before the Lord and say, "You never told me." He is speaking all the time to us; it is our responsibility to listen for Him.

Romans 1:20-21 KJV – *For the invisible things of him from the creation of the world are clearly seen, being understood by the things that are made, even his eternal power and Godhead; so that they are without excuse: Because that, when they knew God, they glorified him not as God, neither were thankful; but became vain in their imaginations, and their foolish heart was darkened.*

When we look at that Scripture passage in Romans 1, we are being told that deep spiritual truth is being conveyed through everyday, ordinary things around us. If we have an eye to see, we will see it. If we have an ear to hear Him, we will hear Him. Our eyes and our ears must be set upon our heart that is set on His heart.

David was a man after God's own heart in such a profound way that he heard God speak to him in everything. God was so moved by David that He put him in grace a thousand years before grace was offered to the rest of humanity. When you start hearing God speak and following Him, you will go to extraordinary places because you are going after His heart.

We hear Him when He is loud. *"The Lord thundered from heaven, and the Most High uttered His voice, hailstones and coals of fire"* (Psalm 18:13). But what if His voice is masked in something else that gets your attention? You have to be willing to hear His voice in the thunder.

> *"Now My soul is troubled, and what shall I say? 'Father, save Me from this hour'? But for this purpose I came to this hour. Father, glorify Your name." When a voice came from heaven, saying, "I have both glorified it and will glorify it again." Therefore the people who stood by and heard it said that it had thundered. Others said, "An angel has spoken to Him." Jesus answered and said, "This voice did not come because of Me, but for your sake. Now is the judgment of this world; now*

the ruler of this world will be cast out. And I, if I am lifted up from the earth, will draw all peoples to Myself." This He said, *signifying by what death He would die* (John 12:27-33 NKJV).

We find in this John 12 Scripture passage a time when Jesus is having a human moment. There are a lot of places in His heart and in His Spirit and in His flesh and His mind and emotions and understanding, and they are not all jiving. So He says:

Now My soul is troubled, and what shall I say? "Father, save Me from this hour"? But for this purpose I came to this hour.

Jesus is saying, "It is not all good, everything is not great, I can't say I'm happy about everything, I can't say I'm loving this moment. I don't know what else to say except: *Father, glorify Your name.*'"

The next verse says, "*Then a voice came from heaven, saying, 'I have both glorified it and will glorify it again.*'"

This is a voice of confidence coming to Jesus, saying He is doing it. His Father is saying He has done it, and He is going to do it again. Likewise, you may be feeling like nothing good is happening, but that is not the case. It is game on!

The Father is saying this to Jesus and the Bible is giving us a glimpse into this exchange between the Divinity of the Father and the humanity of Jesus. We get to see it because there are times when we are so human that we don't know how to do anything except glorify His name. What does it mean to glorify His name? It means to make a big deal about how you personally know Him. When we aren't happy about our situation, we can decide to make a big deal out of the way that we know Him.

> *Therefore, the people who had stood by and heard it, said it had thundered. Others said, "An angel has spoken to Him."*

This is a dramatic moment. This is Jesus being vulnerable and saying, "My soul," which is His mind, will, and emotions, "is not in sync with the hour I am in right now, and I need help." And God Almighty is responding in the most kind, confident, fatherly way, which is awesome. There is something amazingly supernatural happening in the midst of something natural. Some people only saw the natural and never saw the supernatural.

There is a very dangerous group in this, too. There is a group who knew God was moving and that He was speaking, but they didn't have a clue what was being said or who was saying it, so they came up with their own story. They said it was angels talking. They weren't willing to search out the matter, so they came up with their own made-up story.

John gives us wise counsel in his first epistle about such people:

> *Beloved, do not believe every spirit, but test the spirits, whether they are of God; because many false prophets have gone out into the world. By this you know the Spirit of God: Every spirit that confesses that Jesus Christ has come in the flesh is of God, and every spirit that does not confess that Jesus Christ has come in the flesh is not of God. And this is the spirit of the Antichrist, which you have heard was coming, and is now already in the world.*

You are of God, little children, and have overcome them, because He who is in you is greater than he who is in the world. They are of the world. Therefore they speak as of the world, and the world hears them. We are of God. He who knows God hears us; he who is not of God does not hear us. By this we know the spirit of truth and the spirit of error (1 John 4:1-6 NKJV).

We must know God personally. We hear God; that is how we know we are Christians. He is the One we seek direction from, not those who are of the world.

Sometimes the volume of God is a whisper that is as loud as thunder. Sometimes He is supernaturally speaking through a natural event. Sometimes He is speaking through a thunderous event. God is not limited in what He can speak through.

The still, small voice can only be heard by people who are still and small before the Lord. Let's get still, and let's get small. Let's have so much value for His voice that no matter what we are doing, we know God isn't afraid of getting into it with us, so we can hear Him. God is broadcasting His voice to the whole world.

Do not let the mainstream media or Hollywood direct the narrative of your life. A negative narrative doesn't work for us anymore. Remember the 2016 election and the Steve Harvey debacle? What if we look at that and ask, "If that were a dream, what would it mean?" The way we get good at interpreting our dreams is to be good at seeing God in absolutely everything around us.

In summary of that event, on live television, Steve Harvey announced that the contestant from Colombia had won the Miss Universe Pageant. She walked onto the stage and began receiving all the accolades and fanfare with regal music playing and the crown being prepared for her.

Then Steve Harvey says, "Oh, I'm so sorry!" The look on his face was profoundly sorry. He came to the front and said, "This is my fault; it isn't anybody else's fault. I misread this. I'm sorry, it doesn't say Miss Colombia is the winner. It says in the fine print that Miss Colombia is the runner-up." Then, in an awkward and painful moment, he explains that Miss Philippines has won, so the crown was taken back to be given to the real winner. The accolades and fanfare were then resumed for the rightful winner.

In that dramatic, cultural event, God was speaking. Eleven months later, for one shining moment, Hillary Clinton was crowned by Hollywood and the celebrity left as the president of the United States of America. Then the press began announcing they had made a terrible mistake. Trump, the man famous for, among other things, owning the Miss Universe Pageant, took the crown as the president of the United States after a tremendous misread by the press.

I told everyone a long time before the election that the Miss Universe Pageant debacle had to do with the election. The word the Lord had given me was "Great Confusion." At the time I didn't know what that meant when God gave me that word. That's the way prophetic messages are. Anything prophetic will come in part, and we may not understand it all until after an event happens. You don't get everything in one piece. We see in part.

I gave the words God had given me for the year at the New Beginnings conference. I also gave another two-word phrase, "Great Confusion." On Tuesday morning after the election, as CNN anchors wept at what had happened, this quote went through the ticker tape at the bottom of the screen, "Great Confusion with Mass Media's misinterpretation of pre-election polls." There it was; the word of God came to pass.

God Almighty was delivering a message through the Steve Harvey debacle. It was a thunder that caught everybody's attention, but in it was a whisper. Some said it thundered, but some said the voice of God was in that. It was Steve Harvey who made the announcement, and he handled himself like a pro all the way through it, and he probably never knew he had been a prophetic "type" in this word from God.

Let's search this out. The name Steve means "crowning victory," and that is exactly what the prophetic word was all about. But if you dreamed this, you would have to look up more than that.

If you are lazy, you will never hear God speak. If you are fascinated, you will be in wonder. It is signs, miracles, and wonders. You will be filled with wonder when you are fascinated by God and what He is saying.

So, the name Steve means "crowning victory." In the Greek games, Stephanos was the word for the crown that encircled the head of the one who won a game. It was named for the first martyr, Stephen, who earned the very first martyr's crown. The stoning of Stephen is found in the book of Acts.

The name Harvey tells us why one will win and one will lose. It means a branding iron or a blazing iron. In the Bible, Harvey represents a word of deliverance upon God's people.

Deuteronomy 4:20 NIV – *But as for you, the Lord took you and brought you out of the iron-smelting furnace, out of Egypt, to be the people of his inheritance, as you now are.*

The reason Donald Trump won was for our sake and for the sake of Israel.

When looking at types, we must keep one thing in mind: People who represent evil types in God's narrative may be very fine people, and people who represent very good types may be very evil people.

I believe Miss Colombia is a "type" for the American press. Colombia means the land that Columbus discovered, and her name, Arevalo, means the Great Wall. The American press has villainized Trump over the building of the wall, and their crown has been taken off. They lost, and it was a shaming moment for them on national television, just like the Miss Universe Pageant.

Ten months later, the same thing happened at the highest moment of Hollywood. At the Academy Awards there was another situation just like these two. During the show when it was time to announce the very highest award, Best Picture, Warren Beatty got up on stage with Faye Dunaway to announce the winner. They had been picked to do this because it was the anniversary of the movie *Bonnie and Clyde*. So they announced that the Best Picture of the best of what Hollywood had was *La La Land*, which is about Hollywood.

Then, reminiscent of Steve Harvey, after the award had been presented, they had to make the announcement that they were wrong. They had to take the award back because it belonged to the movie *Moonlight*. We are dealing with the titles and types as we seek this out. All the way through Scripture, moonlight represents the testimony of the church. *La La Land* represents Hollywood, and *Moonlight* represents the church. The moon doesn't have any light; it can only reflect the light of the sun. The church can only reflect the light of the Son.

Individually, we don't have any light; we can only reflect the light of King Jesus.

Warren Beatty and Faye Dunaway were up there representing *Bonnie and Clyde.* That reflects what God thinks of Hollywood; they are a bunch of thieves and gangsters who intimidate and scare people. They demand people do what they want and tell them there is nothing they can do about it.

Donald Trump was exactly 70 years, 7 months, and 7 days old on his first full day as President of the United States, and that happened during the year 5777 on the Hebrew calendar.

He had the number stamped 777 on him on his first day. He is a type. A type that represents a move of God that was supposed to be happening among us.

7 – means the Spirit of God.

This number marks where God is doing something by His Spirit apart from any other source. There's really no reason for the year to be divided up into 7-day increments we call weeks. Why isn't a week 5 days, 10 days, or even 12? There is no reason except the fact that God set it up for us to pay attention to the 7th day from the very beginning.

The true and living God declared that human beings would live with a perspective and awareness of 7. While 6 days belong to hard work, labor, and the trouble we face, there has always been, from the very beginning, hope for the 7th day.

God wants us to put our hope in Him. The first understanding that anyone ever had of God after the fall of Adam was for hope of rest on the day that God gave preeminence. That's the basic standard for what 7 represents. Seven is where the Spirit of God brings us hope and something to look forward to—a day that was promised and even commanded. Seven represents something that would surely come to pass. It all has to do with the Spirit of God wrapping something up or perfecting it. God intended for Trump to become president because God knew he would accomplish some of God's desires for the United States and for Israel.

DREAMS

We spend one-third of our lives sleeping. God, however, does not sleep.

> *He will not allow your foot to be moved; He who keeps you will not slumber. Behold, He who keeps Israel shall neither slumber nor sleep* (Psalm 121:3-4 NKJV).

God Almighty wants to invade the sleeping part of our lives. He speaks prophetically to us through the dreams He gives us. He wants us to become skilled in hearing Him in all the ways He speaks to us, including searching out the meaning of dreams.

The Scriptures speak to the importance of hearing and seeing God through the dreams and visions He gives us. Through His prophet Joel, when God wanted His people to know that He was in the midst of them, He said,

> *And it shall come to pass afterward that I will pour out My Spirit on all flesh; your sons and your daughters shall prophesy, your old men shall dream dreams, your young men shall see visions* (Joel 2:28 NKJV).

There is a progression of how we receive dreams shown in this verse in Joel 2. The dreams come to sons and daughters. When it refers to old men, the word is referring to the spiritually mature. It doesn't mean old according to the calendar; rather, it means mature in their walk with the Lord. They have a depth of knowledge of Scripture, so they are given dreams they can interpret with wisdom based on Scripture. The young in faith have visions. They don't yet have the depth of Scripture, but God wants them to seek out and understand what He will show them.

The progression can be understood as the progression of the release of a new movie that is coming. The vision is like a movie preview, it gives you an idea of the movie's content. A dream is like seeing a scene from the movie. And when the prophecy comes into reality, it is like seeing a movie unfold before your eyes.

Dreams don't just happen. It takes work. You must write them down, pray into them for wisdom and understanding, then decree them and declare them. Then you have to put feet to your dreams. You can't just say, "I had a dream and if God wants this to happen, He will make it happen." God has done His part. He is saying to you, "Now, you be My hands, you be My feet; go forth and see this into reality."

When we have dreams, they can be a green light, an invitation, or a commandment to seek God in a certain way or to walk with God in a certain way. Many times, it is because He has a new thing He wants to do in our lives.

I had a dream a couple of years ago that resulted in us beginning a new work that we are still doing today. In my dream, a woman came up to me and said, "Hello, Pastor Troy. Do you know who I am?" I answered, "No, ma'am." Then she said, "I am Nicaragua. Come and feed me." When I saw her, I started tearing up. She was so beautiful, and I knew that Jesus loved her so much. If she had been in the natural, she would have been absolutely gorgeous, but she was also incredibly skinny. She was near death because she had been starving for so long.

I knew this dream was from the Lord. I began to pray, asking the Lord to show me His plan. This dream gave me a desire to respond quickly to what the Lord had shown me. Two months later, I was in our church tuning up my guitar when a man walked in front of me. As I looked at him, I knew I knew that man, but I couldn't remember how. A minute later, Pastor Les brought the man back to me and said, "Hey, Troy, this is Pastor Roger." I interrupted him because I immediately remembered who he was. This was a man who was in Nicaragua, and I had stayed with him at his house over 20 years earlier. We were so happy to reconnect.

He said, "Pastor Troy, I love you!" That feeling was mutual as memories of him returned to me. That day, we began a partnership that led to building a food bank in Nicaragua. The fact that we were reconnected to Pastor Roger was a miracle. Because I didn't ignore the dream, God continued to show me how He wanted to work through me to bring it into reality.

That was a new thing we did in Nicaragua, but it was similar to other things the Lord had us do. Sometimes the Lord brings very new things to be done as well. You may get a dream that is a profound dream, but it may not begin to happen for quite a while. It is very important to keep a journal. Keep it where you can write in it when you first wake up from a dream. The lie is, "Oh, I'll remember that." But you won't. The enemy of God's Kingdom doesn't want you to.

Write it down immediately with every detail in the dream. God will prompt you to recall it when the time is right.

SHADOWS

There is much said in the Scriptures about shadows.

Usually, the phrase "types and shadows" refers to a foreshadowing of things to come, which reflects the things that were. As our awareness of making sure we are hearing all that God wants to say to us increases, we will see more in Scripture.

THE PASSOVER LAMB

The Passover Lamb clearly shows a type and shadow.

God commanded the Israelites to sacrifice an unblemished lamb when they were in captivity in Egypt. He was going to release the last plague on the Egyptians and release the spirit of death to kill their firstborn sons. God's people were given clear instructions on how to make their sacrifice. They were to sprinkle the blood of the lamb on the doorposts of their homes. When God saw the blood of the lamb on the doorpost, He would "pass over" that home and prevent death from happening.

They were also told to be ready to leave so they could escape bondage forever.

Jesus became the sacrifice for us like the Passover Lamb was for the Israelites. He is without sin, and it is His blood that God sees when He looks at us. Because of His blood, we stand forgiven and washed white as the unblemished lamb's wool.

Jesus is depicted as the Lamb in the New Testament. John the Baptist identifies Jesus by saying, ...*"Behold! The Lamb of God who takes away the sin of the world!"* (John 1:29 NKJV).

The apostle Paul often uses types and shadows to help the first believers understand that Jesus was the fulfillment of what God was doing; He was not abandoning the old. One example is when he states, *"...For indeed Christ, our Passover, was sacrificed for us"* (1 Corinthians 5:7 NKJV).

Peter says we are redeemed by *"...the precious blood of Christ, the sinless, spotless Lamb of God"* (1 Peter 1:19 NLT).

And looking further into the future, we see in Revelation 5:6 (NKJV), *"...in the midst of the throne and of the four living creatures, and in the midst of the elders, stood a Lamb as though it had been slain...."*

Then we also see the angels, living creatures, and thousands of elders by the throne saying, *"Worthy is the Lamb who was slain to receive power and riches and wisdom, and strength and honor and glory and blessing!"* (Revelation 5:12 NKJV).

There are many types and shadows to search out, including the Feast System, the Festival System, and the Sabbatical System. They are all types of shadows of things to come. God is light, and when He hits His initial object many times, He casts a shadow over things.

> *So let no one judge you in food or in drink, or regarding a festival or a new moon or sabbaths, which are a shadow of things to come, but the substance is of Christ* (Colossians 2:16-17 NKJV).

In the book of Hebrews, we find a clear and beautiful description of a biblical understanding of the use of the word shadow.

Here is the main point: We have a High Priest who sat down in the place of honor beside the throne of the majestic God in heaven. There he ministers in the heavenly Tabernacle, the true place of worship that was built by the Lord and not by human hands.

And since every high priest is required to offer gifts and sacrifices, our High Priest must make an offering, too. If he were here on earth, he would not even be a priest, since there already are priests who offer the gifts required by the law. They serve in a system of worship that is only a copy, a shadow of the real one in heaven. For when Moses was getting ready to build the Tabernacle, God gave him this warning: "Be sure that you make everything according to the pattern I have shown you here on the mountain."

But now Jesus, our High Priest, has been given a ministry that is far superior to the old priesthood, for he is the one who mediates for us a far better covenant with God, based on better promises (Hebrews 8:1-6 NLT).

Understanding types and shadows and the meaning of numbers is not something we look at for heady knowledge or interesting facts. It is also not about the fascination of studying various types or interesting ways numbers speak to us. We don't seek to be prophetic so we can amaze people with our dreams.

The point of all of this is to bring us closer to our Father. The desire of His heart since He placed humankind on the ground in Eden has been to be our God and for us to be His people. He wants us to be people who invite Him to live among us so He can walk with us and talk with us. Remembering what He has spoken to His people in the past honors Him. Learning to hear Him in all the ways He is speaking to us draws us in closer to Him. Seeing Him in His world shows us more about His nature and character than we will understand if we aren't looking for it.

In coming to understand His nature and character, we grow in our understanding of what nature and character we should have as we are more and more transformed into His likeness every day. As we walk that out, we will show the world that Jesus takes very ordinary people and does extraordinary things through them. In that revelation, perhaps they will also have a deep desire to know Him.

Delighting ourselves in our time with Him and listening with wonder in our soul to what He is saying to us shows Him how much we love Him, and that brings Him joy. Can there be any higher purpose than to love the One who loves us so much?

NOTE

1   Rick Joyner, *The Harvest* (Fort Mill, SC: Morningstar Publication, 2007).

LAST WORDS

In conclusion, I can see throughout history that God has always been speaking. Therefore, it encourages me to always hear God speak in the right now and to have hope for what God is speaking about my future. Turns out we need to be really good at hope these days.

Even as we look at the terrible tragedies of the past and the hopeful dreams of our future, our hope always has to be focused on Jesus and the heart of the Father. That really is His word. The prophetic is not just about telling the future, and it's not only about what's going to happen. The prophetic is about knowing the heart of the Father. Just because something terrible happens doesn't mean that God's amazing heart cannot be heard within it—in fact, that is one of the most important times when we need to be able to hear Him clearly.

I hope that this book has helped you and will continue to help you to have this conversation with your friends, your family, your neighbors, and the people you come across. There will be times when you can say, "Hey, do you see this event over there? Well, the Kingdom of Heaven is just like that!"

Troy

Addendum

The following are two easy-to-use reference guides to strengthen your prophetic skill set:

1. Numbers That Preach and Their Meanings
2. Dream Interpretation Guide

Numbers That Preach and Their Meaning

1 – Unity:

This number also has to do with Superiority, Priority, Beginnings, and God Himself.

> Genesis 1:1 (NKJV) – *In the beginning, God created the heavens and the earth.*

> John 1:1 (NKJV) – *In the beginning was the Word, and the Word was with God, and the Word was God.*

2 – A Faithful Witness and Being Set Apart:

This number also has to do with manifest power, testimony, being made separate, and godly division.

In the negative, it tends to represent what believers should be separate from and a witness to.

Words that only appear twice throughout the entire Word of God tend to be associated with things the Word is a witness against or separated from.

> Revelation 11:3 (NKJV) – *And I will give power unto my **two** witnesses, and they shall prophesy one thousand two hundred and sixty days, clothed in sackcloth.*

3 – Perfect Completion:

This number illustrates fullness and being complete. Three is the resurrection and the number God stamps on divinity.

> Exodus 19:11 (NKJV) – *"...For on the third day the Lord will come down upon Mount Sinai in the sight of all the people."*

> Luke 24:46 (NKJV) – *Then He said to them, "Thus it is written, and thus it was necessary for the Christ to suffer and to rise from the dead the third day."*

4 – Creation and Things That Are Made:

This number has to do with things that are made. Four is the "world" number—the number God stamps on things that have to do with "all the world" within His creations.

In the negative, it represents worldliness and worldly systems.

Words that occur four times in Scripture: lost, thin, afflicted, ignorance, fault, wages

> Matthew 24:14 (NKJV) – *And this gospel of the kingdom shall be preached in **all the world** for a witness unto all nations; and then the end will come.*

5 – THE GRACE OF GOD:

Five also has to do with the favor of God. It is the number that marks the place where God gives us the ability to overcome something.

Ephesians 2:8 (NKJV) – *For by grace you have been saved through faith, and that not of yourselves; it is the gift of God.*

6 – THE FLESH OF MAN:

This number also has to do with man's opposition to God and man's pitiful stance against God.

Romans 6:6 (NKJV) – *Knowing this, that our old **man** is crucified with Him, that the body of sin might be done away with, that we should no longer be slaves of sin.*

7 – THE SPIRIT OF GOD:

The number 7 marks where God is doing something by His Spirit apart from any other source. It is the number that marks His rest and where He rules over all things created. Seven is perfection of Spirit.

Deuteronomy 28:7 (NKJV) – *The Lord will cause your enemies who rise against you to be defeated before your face; they shall come out against you one way and flee before you seven ways.*

Matthew 18:21-22 (NKJV) – *Then Peter came to Him and said, "Lord, how often shall my brother sin against me, and I forgive him? Up to seven times?" Jesus said to him, "I do not say to you, up to seven times, but up to seventy times seven."*

8 – New Beginnings:

Eight is the number God uses to illustrate resurrection. It has to do with new birth, new life, and new creation.

> Revelation 21:5 (NKJV) – *Then He who sat on the throne said, "Behold, I make all things new."*

9 – Fruit Bearing:

Nine represents the Spirit bearing fruit and forward progression. Examples of 9 in Scripture as Fruit Bearing:

- A woman is pregnant for 9 months before giving birth to new life.

- Life is a great gift as John 3:16 declares.

- There are 9 gifts of the Spirit made manifest when God's judgment is life: love, joy, peace, patience, kindness, goodness, faithfulness, gentleness, and self-control.

- Jesus Christ died on the cross at the 9th hour and would become the firstfruits of the resurrected.

> 1 Corinthians 15:20 (NKJV) – *But now Christ is risen from the dead, and has become the firstfruits of those who have fallen asleep.*

9 – In the negative means Judgment, with emphasis on the judgment being by the Spirit of God.

- All forms of the word "death" appear 999 times in the Bible.

- There are 9 biblical sieges of Jerusalem.

- In Haggai chapter 1, God's judgment is poured out upon 9 different things.

10 – PERFECT ORDER:

This number has to do with timelines and how God carries out a plan in perfect order.

> Deuteronomy 4:13 (NKJV) – *He declared to you His covenant which He commanded you to perform, the Ten Commandments; and He wrote them on two tablets of stone.*

11 – HEROES RISING:

Eleven stands out as marking where God recognizes the faithfulness of people. Eleven is associated with valor and notable acts of selfless service.

11 – In the negative means Disorder. The number 11 represents judgment, with an emphasis on the disorder.

> Jeremiah 11:11 (NKJV) – *Therefore thus says the Lord: "Behold, I will surely bring calamity on them which they will not be able to escape; and though they cry out to Me, I will not listen to them."*

It's not the numbers people need to see but the Word of God that the numbers point to. God is preaching through the number 11; and when He does, He usually tells us we are out of order and out from under His protection.

Any person, government, or any part of a person's life that is not under King Jesus as the head is out of order. It's all about vertical alignment.

Judgment, Disorder, and the United States

There have been many 11s stamped on national American tragedies throughout our history:

- On 11/11/1778, loyalists to England and local Indians massacred 42 American settlers at Cherry Valley, New York. It sent our fledgling nation into shock.

- President Lincoln's final public speech was given on April 11, 1865, just 3 days before his assassination.

- But there is no greater 11 associated with American tragedies than that of 9/11.

12 – PERFECT GOVERNMENT:

Twelve is the last of 4 numbers God uses to show His perfection. It's the number that shows God is in control and actively ruling over something as King.

> Matthew 26:53 (NKJV) – *Do you think that I cannot now pray to My Father, and He will provide Me with more than twelve legions of angels?*

13 – REBELLION:

Thirteen is the number most closely associated with apostasy.

> Genesis 13:13 (NKJV) – *But the men of Sodom were exceedingly wicked and sinful against the Lord.*

14 – Generational Promises and the Fear of the Lord:

The fear of the Lord is to love what God loves and hate what He hates. This number points to the Spirit made manifest.

> Matthew 1:17 (NKJV) – *So all the generations from Abraham to David are fourteen generations, from David until the captivity in Babylon are fourteen generations, and from the captivity in Babylon until the Christ are fourteen generations.*

15 – Rest and Overcoming Death:

Fifteen is 3 x 5. Three represents "perfect completion," and 5 represents "grace" or "God-given ability to overcome something."

Hezekiah cried to the Lord and was given 15 years more years to live, so he overcame death and God delivered him from his enemy.

> 2 Kings 20:6 (NKJV) – *I will add to your days fifteen years. I will deliver you and this city from the hand of the king of Assyria; and I will defend this city for My own sake, and for the sake of My servant David.*

16 – The Love of God:

All new beginnings happen because of the love of God. Sixteen is the number God uses to identify His love toward us.

> John 3:16 (NKJV) – *For God so loved the world that He gave His only begotten Son, that whoever believes in Him should not perish but have everlasting life.*

17 – OVERCOMING VICTORY:

It's the number given to those who overcome. Just like that, the number 34 (17 x 2) is when God manifests His overcoming power.

> 1 John 5:4-5 (NKJV) – *For whatever is born of God overcomes the world. And this is the victory that has overcome the world— our faith. Who is he who overcomes the world, but he who believes that Jesus is the Son of God?*

18 – LIFE MORE ABUNDANTLY:

Eighteen is the number that represents life in Christ for the believer-multiplying life.

In the negative – The Bondage of Sin. In the negative, the number 18 (3 x 6 or "man, man, man") is associated very closely with the *Flesh*.

> Matthew 18:18 (NKJV) – *Assuredly, I say to you, whatever you bind on earth will be bound in heaven, and whatever you loose on earth will be loosed in heaven.*

19 – FAITH:

There are 19 examples of faith in Hebrews 11, and faith comes by hearing.

Zacchaeus encountered Jesus and believed:

> Luke 19:9-10 (NKJV) – *And Jesus said to him, "Today salvation has come to this house, because he also is a son of Abraham; for the Son of Man has come to seek and to save that which was lost."*

Acts 19:4-5 (NKJV) – *Then Paul said, "John indeed baptized with a baptism of repentance, saying to the people that they should believe on Him who would come after him, that is, on Christ Jesus." When they heard this, they were baptized in the name of the Lord Jesus.*

20 – Expectancy and Redemption:

Twenty is the number associated with hopeful waiting, expectancy fulfilled, and God bringing redemption into broken places.

Jude 1:20-21 (NIV) – *But you, dear friends, by building yourselves up in your most holy faith and praying in the Holy Spirit, keep yourselves in God's love as you wait for the mercy of our Lord Jesus Christ to bring you to eternal life.*

21 – Manifest Spirit:

Twenty-one is the number formed from 7 x 3. When the Spirit (7) has perfectly completed (3) His work, everything is seen for what it really is.

John 3:21 (NKJV) – *But he who does the truth comes to the light, that his deeds may be clearly seen, that they have been done in God.*

22 – Personal Revelation:

There are 22 chapters in the book of Revelation. Light is used 22 times in the Gospel of John. Jesus is the Light of that world.

In the negative, 22 is the product of 11 x 2; sometimes 22 can mean a witness or manifestation of disorder.

Revelation 22:8 (NKJV) – *Now I, John, saw and heard these things. And when I heard and saw, I fell down to worship before the feet of the angel who showed me these things.*

23 –Being in the Presence of God:

It's the number formed from 10 + 13. In the negative, it's how God brings His perfect order to man's rebellion: judgment of death through the Law. In the positive, it's associated with being in the presence of God.

Jeremiah 23:23 (NIV) – *"Am I only a God nearby," declares the Lord, "and not a God far away?"*

So when God wants to tell us His presence is very near to us, He uses the number 23 to proclaim it.

In the negative – Death.

Romans 1:28-32 (KJV) – *And even as they did not like to retain God in their knowledge, God gave them over to a reprobate mind, to do those things which are not convenient; being filled with all unrighteousness, fornication, wickedness, covetousness, maliciousness; full of envy, murder, debate, deceit, malignity; whisperers, backbiters, haters of God, despiteful, proud, boasters, inventors of evil things, disobedient to parents, without understanding, covenant breakers, without natural affection, implacable, unmerciful: Who knowing the judgment of God, **that they which commit such things are worthy of death....***

These 23 things listed here, by the judgment of the Lord, lead to DEATH.

24 – PERFECT GOVERNMENT MADE MANIFEST:

Twenty-four is the product of 12 x 2 and is connected with God governing something. (See my notes on the number 12 for more information.)

- Many other works and websites say some people attribute the number 24 to intercession and prayer. That makes sense when you line up with the priests and the elders.

- There are 24 priests in 1 Chronicles 24. There are 24 elders in Revelation.

- The 24 divisions of priests (1 Chronicles 24:1-9) and cantors (1 Chronicles 25:9-31).

- There are 24 chapters in the Gospel of Luke.

  Luke 24:44 (NKJV) – *Then He said to them, "These are the words which I spoke to you while I was still with you, that all things must be fulfilled which were written in the Law of Moses and the Prophets and the Psalms concerning Me."*

Encircled and Protected:

- There is a pattern connected to being encircled and protected. Perhaps guarded and watched over.

- The world is 24,000-plus miles around.

- There are 24 hours in a day.

- Interesting fact: there are 37 recorded miracles of Jesus and exactly 24 cures.

25 – Grace for Grace:

Twenty-five is the number of grace (5) multiplied by 5 (5 x 5). Twenty-five means God will perform the things He gave you grace for.

> John 1:16-17 (NKJV) – *And of His fullness we have all received, and grace for grace. For the law was given through Moses, but grace and truth came through Jesus Christ.*

26 – Beloved:

The number 26 has to do with messianic bloodlines and King David. In the book Song of Solomon, written by King David's son, the word *beloved* is found exactly 26 times. The name *David* actually means "beloved." It is the number of generations from David to Christ. It is the numerical value of the name of God in Hebrew. It is the sum of the Hebrew letters yod, he, waw, and he, giving us the name *YHWH*, 10+5+6+5=26.

> Song of Solomon 6:3 (NKJV) – *I am my beloved's, and my beloved is mine.*

27 – Things Unveiled and Revealed in God's Presence, and Light of Truth:

Twenty-seven is 3 to the third power (3 x 3 x 3). It is the revelation of all things Jesus. His candlestick burns bright, and He will not remove it because we will not leave our first love. Progressive revelation and light of truth are connected with 27.

> Matthew 17:2,5 (NKJV) – *And He was transfigured before them. His face shone like the sun, and His clothes became as white as the light. And behold, Moses and Elijah appeared to them, talking with Him. ...Behold, a bright cloud overshadowed them; and suddenly a voice came out of the cloud, saying, "This is My beloved Son, in whom I am well pleased. Hear Him!"*

28 – TIMES AND SEASONS:

Twenty-eight is the number associated with the beginning and the end of certain God-given timelines. Ecclesiastes chapter 3 lists 28 times and seasons for every purpose under Heaven.

> Ecclesiastes 3:1 (NKJV) – *To everything there is a season, and a time to every purpose under the heaven.*

- Twenty-eight times, the word *weeks* appears; a measure of time.
- The phrase "day and night" appears exactly 28 times throughout Scripture.
- There are 28 days in a lunar month.
- The word *cross* appears exactly 28 times in the Bible.

> Matthew 28:20 (KJV) – *...and, lo, I am with you always, even unto the end of the world. Amen.*

29 – MOUNTAINS:

Since mountains are associated with hearing God speak and the voice of the Lord, the number 29 is also associated with those themes. It could have to do with instruction from the Lord as well, but it definitely has to do with mountains. There are 29 mountains in the Bible.

> Revelation 21:10 (NKJV) – *And he carried me away in the Spirit to a great and high mountain, and showed me the great city, the holy Jerusalem, descending out of heaven from God,*

30 – ACTS OF REDEMPTION AND ACCOMPLISHING PRIESTLY SERVICE:

When there is a Kingdom venture, when Heaven is beginning to transform the earth, God likes to stamp the number 30 on it. When somebody is serving the Lord in a very significant way, God seems to stamp the number 30 on it.

Judas betrayed Jesus for 30 silver coins. Amazingly, not only was this the price for a prime servant (Leviticus 27:1-7), it was a fulfillment of prophecy (Zechariah 11:12).

> Matthew 26:14-15 (NKJV) – *Then one of the twelve, called Judas Iscariot, went to the chief priests and said, "What are you willing to give me if I deliver Him to you?" And they counted out to him thirty pieces of silver.*

31 – OFFSPRING:

The gematria of the word *offspring* is 31. Moses, who was saved as a baby and set apart as a child, is in 31 different books of the Bible. The mother of all nations, Rebecca, is found 31 different times in the Bible. Also, offspring and the number 731: When we see 731 everywhere we look, it might be that God Almighty is speaking to you about the generations behind you. The 731st verse in the Bible is when Jacob took the birthright away from Esau, so there's offspring again.

> Genesis 25:29-33 (NKJV) – *Now Jacob cooked a stew; and Esau came in from the field, and he was weary. And Esau said to Jacob, "Please feed me with that same red stew, for I am weary." Therefore his name was called Edom. But Jacob said, "Sell me your birthright as of this day." And Esau said, "Look, I am about to die; so what is this birthright to me?" Then Jacob said, "Swear to me as of this day." So he swore to him, and sold his birthright to Jacob.*

> 1 John 3:1 (NKJV) – *Behold what manner of love the Father has bestowed on us, that we should be called children of God!*

32 – THE CAMP OF GOD AND THE ROYALTY WITHIN ITS LINEAGE:

Ephesians 2:19 (NKJV) – *Now, therefore, you are no longer strangers and foreigners, but fellow citizens with the saints and members of the household of God.*

1 Peter 2:9 (NKJV) – *But you are a chosen generation, a royal priesthood, a holy nation, His own special people, that you may proclaim the praises of Him who called you out of darkness into His marvelous light.*

33 – God Keeps His Promises:

1 Kings 8:56 (NLT) – *Praise the Lord who has given rest to his people Israel, just as he promised. Not one word has failed of all the wonderful promises he gave through his servant Moses.*

2 Corinthians 1:20 (NIV) – *For no matter how many promises God has made, they are "Yes" in Christ. And so through him the "Amen" is spoken by us to the glory of God.*

34 – Identification and Time to Overcome or God's Overcoming Victory Through His Miracles:

1 John 5:4-5 (NKJV) – *For whatever is born of God overcomes the world. And this is the victory that has overcome the world— our faith. Who is he who overcomes the world, but he who believes that Jesus is the Son of God?*

35 – Authority Inspiration and Leading of the Holy Spirit:

Romans 8:14 (NKJV) – *For as many as are led by the Spirit of God, these are sons of God.*

37 – Don't Worry, Be Happy:

John 15:10-11 (NKJV) – *If you keep My commandments, you will abide in My love, just as I have kept My Father's commandments and abide in His love. These things I have spoken to you, that My joy may remain in you, and that your joy may be full.*

38 – Getting Back into God's Will When You're in Trouble:

Acts 2:38 (NKJV) – *Then Peter said to them, "Repent, and let every one of you be baptized in the name of Jesus Christ for the remission of sins; and you shall receive the gift of the Holy Spirit."*

39 – Rebellion, Rebellion Complete (13 x 3), and Receiving Rebellion:

Psalm 39:8 (NLT) – *Rescue me from my rebellion. Do not let fools mock me.*

40 – Pass the Test, Trials, Testing, and Probation:

Forty is clearly defined throughout Scripture. It is the number for *trial* or a *probation time.*

The dictionary defines *probation* as:

1. The act of testing.
2. The testing or trial of a person's conduct, character, qualifications, etc.
3. The state or period of such testing or trial.

Matthew 4:1-3 (NKJV) – *Then Jesus was led up by the Spirit into the wilderness to be tempted by the devil. And when He had fasted forty days and forty nights, afterward He was hungry. Now when the tempter came to Him, he said, "If You are the Son of God, command that these stones become bread."*

44 – Double Portion of Revelation Light:

Psalm 44:3 (NLT) – *They did not conquer the land with their swords; it was not their own strong arm that gave them victory. It was your right hand and strong arm and the blinding light from your face that helped them, for you loved them.*

45 – Provision, Protection, and Preservation:

Isaiah 45:14 (NKJV) – *Thus says the Lord: "The labor of Egypt and merchandise of Cush and of the Sabeans, men of stature, shall come over to you, and they shall be yours; they shall walk behind you, they shall come over in chains; and they shall bow down to you. They will make supplication to you, saying, 'Surely God is in you, and there is no other; there is no other God.'"*

50 – Jubilee:

Jubilee is when what was taken from you is returned to you. It is also connected with the Holy Spirit, as the Holy Spirit fell on mankind 50 days after the Passover, or on Pentecost.

Leviticus 25:11-12 (NKJV) – *That fiftieth year shall be a Jubilee to you; in it you shall neither sow nor reap what grows of its own accord, nor gather the grapes of your untended vine. For it is the Jubilee; it shall be holy to you; you shall eat its produce from the field.*

51 – Progression, Upgrade, and Restoration:

Psalm 51:7-11 (NKJV) – *Purge me with hyssop, and I shall be clean; wash me, and I shall be whiter than snow. Make me hear joy and gladness, that the bones You have broken may rejoice.*

Hide Your face from my sins, and blot out all my iniquities. Create in me a clean heart, O God, and renew a steadfast spirit within me. Do not cast me away from Your presence, and do not take Your Holy Spirit from me.

52 – Work of God:

Isaiah 52:12 (NKJV) – *For you shall not go out with haste, nor go by flight; for the Lord will go before you, and the God of Israel will be your rear guard.*

53 – Dual Nature of Jesus:

Isaiah 53:2 (NKJV) – *For He shall grow up before Him as a tender plant, and as a root out of dry ground. He has no form or comeliness; and when we see Him, there is no beauty that we should desire Him.*

John 1:1-4,10 (NKJV) – *In the beginning was the Word, and the Word was with God, and the Word was God. He was in the beginning with God. All things were made through Him, and without Him, nothing was made that was made. In Him was life, and the life was the light of men. ...He was in the world, and the world was made through Him, and the world did not know Him.*

66 – A Witness to the Flesh:

The number 6 is all about "man." When doubled, as in 66, they are about being a witness to something. So, the number is associated with a human being having a testimony, possibly against itself.

John 5:39 (NLT) – *Your search the Scriptures because you think they give you eternal life. But the Scriptures point to me!*

John 6:66 (NKJV) – *From that time many of His disciples went back and walked with Him no more.*

70 – KINGDOM OF GOD:

John 18:36 (NKJV) – *Jesus answered, "My kingdom is not of this world. If My kingdom were of this world, My servants would fight, so that I should not be delivered to the Jews; but now My kingdom is not from here."*

Numbers 11:16-17 (NKJV) – *So the Lord said to Moses: "Gather to Me seventy men of the elders of Israel, whom you know to be the elders of the people and officers over them; bring them to the tabernacle of meeting, that they may stand there with you. Then I will come down and talk with you there. I will take of the Spirit that is upon you and will put the same upon them; and they shall bear the burden of the people with you, that you may not bear it yourself alone."*

120 – GOD SHOWS UP AND CHANGES EVERYTHING:

Testing is finished, and God shows up! This number has something to do with completing a process and graduating to better things.

Matthew 1:20 (NKJV) – *But while he thought about these things, behold, an angel of the Lord appeared to him in a dream, saying, "Joseph, son of David, do not be afraid to take to you Mary your wife, for that which is conceived in her is of the Holy Spirit."*

153 – Progression, Upgrade, and Restoration:

John 21:1-7 (NKJV) – *After these things Jesus showed Himself again to the disciples at the Sea of Tiberias, and in this way He showed Himself: Simon Peter, Thomas called the Twin, Nathanael of Cana in Galilee, the sons of Zebedee, and two others of His disciples were together. Simon Peter said to them, "I am going fishing." They said to him, "We are going with you also." They went out and immediately got into the boat, and that night they caught nothing.*

But when the morning had now come, Jesus stood on the shore; yet the disciples did not know that it was Jesus. Then Jesus said to them, "Children, have you any food?"

They answered Him, "No." And He said to them, "Cast the net on the right side of the boat, and you will find some." So they cast, and now they were not able to draw it in because of the multitude of fish. Therefore that disciple whom Jesus loved said to Peter, "It is the Lord!"

199 – Righteousness or Fear of the Lord:

Psalm 19:9-10 (NKJV) – *The fear of the Lord is clean, enduring forever; the judgments of the Lord are true and righteous altogether. More to be desired are they than gold, yea, than much fine gold; sweeter also than honey and the honeycomb.*

300 – Supernatural Deliverance:

Psalm 30:3 (NKJV) – *O Lord, You brought my soul up from the grave; You have kept me alive, that I should not go down to the pit.*

310 – CRYING OUT FOR DELIVERANCE AND DEPENDENCY ON THE LORD:

Revelation 3:10 (NKJV) – *Because you have kept My command to persevere, I also will keep you from the hour of trial which shall come upon the whole world, to test those who dwell on the earth.*

316 – COMPLETE LOVE OF GOD:

John 3:16 (NKJV) – *For God so loved the world that He gave His only begotten Son, that whoever believes in Him should not perish but have everlasting life.*

TRIPLICATES

When a number in the Bible appears in triplicate, such as 666 or 999, it illustrates the total completeness of what the single digit represents. For example, if the number 1 represents unity, the number 111 represents either unity being completed or the presence of total unity. It's no wonder the number 111 is the biblical number for Jehovah God.

111 – TOTAL UNITY:

God's number is 111. God is "The One." When He shows up in 111, it means all 3 persons of Him, the Trinity, are made manifest in fullness.

1 Corinthians 12:1-11 (NKJV) – Explains the unity in the body of Christ.

Hosea 1:11 (NKJV) – *Then the children of Judah and the children of Israel shall be gathered together, and appoint for themselves one head; and they shall come up out of the land, for great will be the day of Jezreel!*

Ephesians 1:10-11 (NKJV) – *That in the dispensation of the fullness of the times He might gather together in one all things in Christ, both which are in heaven and which are on earth—in Him. In Him also we have obtained an inheritance, being predestined according to the purpose of Him who works all things according to the counsel of His will.*

222 - A COMPLETE WITNESS:

The *gematria* of the 3-word term "John the Baptist" is exactly 222, which means that John the Baptist is the perfect and complete witness to Jesus.

222 – SIGNS, MIRACLES, AND WONDERS:

The only Scripture in the entire Bible that has all 3 words "signs," "miracles," and "wonders" is found in Acts 2:22.

Acts 2:22 (NKJV) – *Men of Israel, hear these words: Jesus of Nazareth, a Man attested by God to you by miracles, wonders, and signs which God did through Him in your midst, as you yourselves also know.*

If you are frequently seeing 222, it may be a witness to the manifest power of God, and He wants you to go after Him for it.

222 – INTIMACY AND UNITY:

Perhaps He is speaking to you about a mind-blowing word of intimacy.

Genesis 2:22 (NKJV) – *Then the rib which the Lord God had taken from man He made into a woman, and He brought her to the man.*

222 – AMERICAN REVIVAL:

American revivals tend to be poured out on dates with the number 222. History shows that on 2/22/1906, black evangelist William J. Seymour arrived in the city of angels—Los Angeles, California—and the Azusa Street Revival, the greatest move of the Holy Spirit on this side of the world began. Maybe it's an American thing because 1776, our nation's birthday, is 2x2x2x222 and George Washington's birthday is 2/22/1732.

333 - LEARNING WHAT YOU DON'T KNOW; CRYING OUT TO GOD FOR SOMETHING YOU URGENTLY NEED

Jeremiah 33:3 (NKJV) – *Call to Me, and I will answer you, and show you great and mighty things, which you do not know.*

444 - COMPLETE CREATION, THE WORLD, THE KEY OF DAVID

Word 444 in the New Testament lexicon is: **444** *anthropos*, which means "man," a generic name distinction from gods and animals. The number of the world.

There are 4,440 verses in the 5 major Old Testament prophets books. It's interesting to note that 4,440 ÷ 5 = 888. In other words, when you introduce grace to the prophets, what you get is Jesus because 888 is the *gematria* of the name *Jesus!*

Revelation 3:7 (NKJV) – *And to the angel of the church in Philadelphia write, "These things says He who is holy, He who is true, 'He who has the key of David, He who opens and no one shuts, and shuts and no one opens.'"*

The key of David is a remarkable mystery throughout the Word of God that obviously is connected to the throne of David, and it gains or stops supernatural access to things. Jesus says He holds the key of David. So not only is Jesus the door, Jesus is also the key to the door. A big part of the favor that the Lord has upon you will be demonstrated through the doors that He opens.

There is actually a sound now every time God comes back and changes anything. The sound is a chord set in the key of David, which is tuned at 444 Hz.

Prophetic Voice of Knocking

Supernatural Access: If you hear a knocking sound at random times, it may be that God Almighty wants to talk to you about supernatural access He has waiting for you.

Isaiah 22:22 (NKJV) – *The key of the house of David I will lay on his shoulder; so he shall open, and no one shall shut; and he shall shut, and no one shall open.*

555 - COMPLETE GRACE:

The word *Christ* is found exactly 555 times in the King James New Testament. It is by His complete grace that anyone ever finds Christ. It's in the Bible 555 times!

Isaiah 55:5 *Surely you shall call a nation you do not know, and nations who do not know you shall run to you, because of the Lord your God, and the Holy One of Israel; for He has glorified you.*

666 - Complete Flesh

This is the "mark of the beast." An animal, or a beast, has no concept of God. Spiritual and moral values are of no meaning to it. The number 6 represents man without God. The number 666 means *"man, man, man"* or *"flesh, flesh, flesh."*

The tribulation world system will be totally man-centered, man-dominated, and man-subjugated. Everything in it will be based on man's animalistic thoughts, plans, actions, and schemes. There is no room for God in 666. People will be total flesh, and that's why everyone is forced to wear the mark.

Revelation 13:18 (NKJV) – *Here is wisdom. Let him who has understanding calculate the number of the beast, for it is the number of a man: His number is 666.*

777 - Complete Perfection of Spirit

- Lamech, the father of Noah, was 777 years old when he died.

- There are 777 verses in the Bible that list cities.

- 7 priests + 7 trumpets + 7 times around equals God's Spirit bringing down Jericho's walls.

Joshua 6:4 (NKJV) – *And seven priests shall bear seven trumpets of rams' horns before the ark. But the seventh day you shall march around the city seven times, and the priests shall blow the trumpets.*

888 – JESUS

The Greek word for Jesus is Ἰησοῦς and is a perfect name, and by perfect mathematical design it adds up to 888 (8 x 111) The gematria is 888. Eight is the number for new beginnings, and Jesus is the One who makes all things brand-new. Eight is also the number for resurrection, and He is the Resurrected Christ.

Phrases that equal 888:

- I am the Lord, I change not; Malachi 3:6
- The Salvation of our God; Psalm 98:3
- The Mercy of the Most High; Psalm 21:7
- My Beloved; Song of Solomon 7:13
- The heavens declare the glory of God; Psalm 19:1
- The third day; John 2:1
- They shall be comforted; Matthew 5:4

Notice a few more words and terms I found that equal 888: Scriptures, Father God Is Real, and Immanuel which means God with us.

1111 – EXTRAORDINARY FAITH:

Hebrews 11:11 (NKJV) – *By faith Sarah herself also received strength to conceive seed, and she bore a child when she was past the age, because she judged Him faithful who had promised.*

DREAM INTERPRETATION GUIDE

REVEALING THE MYSTERIES OF BIBLICAL SYMBOLS AND PARABLES

Because one-third of the Bible is God speaking through dreams, visions, and the prophetic, we can know God still speaks through these voices today. Dreams and visions are just one way He communicates with us, but what is He saying? *"It is the glory of God to conceal a matter, but the glory of kings is to search out a matter"* (Proverbs 25:2 NKJV). You can hear God! Do you have the glory or honor of a king? Ready to search for revelation? Join me in the journey to "hear the voice" of God with these tips:

- **Get up and write it down**. Don't wait! Record every detail including emotions. Title and date your dreams and visions for easy reference.

- **Point of view.** Are you participating, observing or the focus? Is this dream similar to other recent dreams? Is it in two or three parts? Who is it about—you, others, a city, church, or nation?

- **Compare and contrast.** Why this and not that? Why the second floor, not the first? Why a train, not a car?

- **Record colors** of key dream elements and the atmosphere: Light or dark? Bright or dim? Is the carpet red? Is the water clear or dirty? Clothing, eyes, hair, cars—take notice.

- **People in dreams:** Do you know them? How? Were you happy to see them? What are their names? Does the name have a meaning? Are they friend or foe? Are they from the past or present? If they are faceless, is their countenance dark or light? Have they been in other recent dreams?

The following lists are a result of my personal experience and study, and the understanding of godly people much smarter than me, including: Tyler Wolfe, Autumn Mann, John Paul Jackson, Dr. Joe Ibojie, Michal Ann and James Goll, Barbara Lardinais, Sharnael Wolverton, Ira Milligan, Adam F. Thompson and Adrian Beale.

Dream on, my friend!
Pastor Troy

Animals

Alligator: evil from the past, danger, destruction, slander

Bat: witchcraft, unstable, flight, fear

Bear: judgment, strength, evil spirit wants what you have

Polar Bear: religious spirit

Beaver: industrious, busy, diligent, clever

Bird: spirits, good or evil

Bull: intimidation, spiritual warfare, strong evil spirit

Cat: self-willed, untrainable, unclean spirit, deception

Black Cat: witchcraft

Chicken: fear, cowardice

Hen: (positive) protection, motherhood; (negative) gossip

Rooster: boasting, bragging, proud

Chick: defenseless, innocent

Crab: not easy to approach, claws holding something

Crow/Raven: (positive) God's minister of justice; (negative) confusion, outspoken, envy, strife, hateful

Cow: subsistence, prosperity

Deer: peace, longing

Dog: (positive) loyalty, faithfulness; (negative) unbelievers, hypocrites

Donkey: (positive) gentle strength, burden bearer; (negative) stubborn

Dove: Holy Spirit

Dragon: satan

Dinosaur: old stronghold, demonic, danger from the past

Eagle: prophetic, prophetic calling, heavenly viewpoint

Elephant: invincible, thick-skinned, not easily offended, powerful, old memory, long pregnancy

Fish: human souls

Fox: cunning, evil men, sly or sneaky, steals from you

Frog: spirit of lust, demon, curse, witchcraft

Goat: sinner, unbelief, stubborn, blamed for sin of others

Hawk: predator with good vision, unexpected attack

Horse: power, strength, conquest

Lamb: Jesus (sacrificial lamb), gentle, innocent, humility

Leopard: unchanging, vengeance, predator, danger

Lion: (positive) Jesus, royalty, brave; (negative) satan seeking to destroy

Mice/Rats: devourer, curse, plague

Mole: spiritual blindness, hidden

Monkey: mocking spirit, foolishness, dishonesty, addiction

Mountain Lion: enemy, predator of your soul

Octopus: Jezebel spirit (because of the tentacles)

Ox: slow change, subsistence

Panther: witchcraft, demonic activity, works in darkness

Peacock: pride

Pig: ignorance, hypocrisy, unbelievers, selfish, gluttonous

Raccoon: mischief or rascal, night raider, thief or bandit

Ram: sacrifice

Sheep: God's people, innocent, vulnerable, sacrifice

Skunk: stench, smell, unforgiving, bitterness, bad attitude

Snake: satan, deception, lies, unforgiving or bitterness

White Snake: spirit of religion, occult

Sparrow: small value but precious

Tortoise: slow moving change, steady

Whale: big impact in the things of the Spirit, going deep in the Spirit

Wolf: satan and evil, false ministries or false teachers, predator, working with others

BODY PARTS

Arm: strength, faith

Beard: maturity

Ear: needing to listen; pull on ear symbolic of meddling

Eye: heart, spirit, eyes of the Lord, prophetic gift, perception

Face: character, countenance

Feet: walk, offense, stubborn (unmovable), rebellion (kicking)

Finger: discernment, conviction, works, instruction

Thumb: apostolic

Pointer: prophetic or accusation

Middle: evangelistic

Ring: pastor, commitment

Pinky: teaching

Hair: wisdom, anointing, glory

Bald Head: lacking wisdom

Hand: relationship, healing

Head: authority, thoughts, mind

Immobilized Body Parts: spiritual hindrance, demonic attack

Knee: reverence, humility, bowing down

Nakedness: transparency, humility, humbling season

Neck: (positive) support or strength; (negative) stiff-necked or stubborn

Nose: discernment

Shoulder: bearing burdens, leadership

Side: relationship, friendship

Teeth: wisdom, understanding, consuming power

Eye Teeth: revelatory understanding

Wisdom Teeth: ability to act in wisdom
Thigh: faith

Buildings* and Places

*Note the size and purpose of the building.

Amphitheater: something will be magnified

Apartment: what you're going through is common to humanity

Atrium: light and growth from Heaven

Garden: love, intimacy, growth

Auto Repair Shop: ministry restoration, renewal, repair

Barn/Warehouse: a place of provision and storage

Castle: authority, fortress, royal residence

City: security, safety, permanence, refuge

Elevator: rising or descending in anointing

Farm: place of provision

Foundation: important foundational and fundamental issues

Fountain: source of life, refreshment

Garage: place of rest and refreshment, place of protection

Gas Station: to receive power

General Store: provision, staples, basics

Hallway: transition

High-Rise Buildings: high spiritual calling or perception

Hospital: place of healing

Hotel: transition, temporary, place to relax or receive

House: a ministry, church, personal life situation or family

Previous Home: past, generational issues

House of Person in Ministry: call to ministry

Two-Story House: double anointing

Mall: (positive) provision, all needs in one place; (negative) materialism

Mobile Home: temporary place or condition, poverty

Office Building: accomplishments

Pasture: place of spiritual nourishment

Porch: place of waiting, place of welcoming

Back Porch: history or past

Front Porch: vision, future

Restaurant: (positive) spiritual feasting; (negative) gluttony

Restaurant Kitchen: preparing spiritual food for others

Roof: covering, oversight

School/Room: training time, teaching anointing, ministry

Shack: poverty

Stadium: place of tremendous impact

Staircase: up or down in the spirit (anointing), portal

Steps: spiritual progress

Tent: temporary place of rest, meeting place with God

Theater: increased notoriety, success

Tunnel: passage, transition, way of escape, hope

Windows: prophetic vision or understanding; letting light in

Wall: fortification, division, refuge

Well: refreshment, source of life

CLOTHING

Bathrobe: coming out of a place of cleansing, spiritual slumber, mantle or anointing

Clothing That Doesn't Fit: walking in something you're not called to, trying to operate in another person's job or calling

Coat: mantle, anointing

Cultural Clothing: calling to another nation, intercession for a particular country or ethnic group

Nakedness: transparency, realness, honesty, natural

Partially Naked: want to be honest, but hiding something

Pajamas: spiritual slumber

Shoes: gospel of peace, bringing good news

Shorts: a walk or calling that is partially fulfilled

Speedo: to move fast in the Spirit

Swimwear: ability to move in the Spirit

Tattered Clothing: anointing not being taken care of

Wedding Dress: covenant, deep relationship

COLORS

Amber: (positive) glory of God; (negative) false glory, self-glorification

Black: (positive) mysterious, unknown; (negative) death, darkness, evil

Blue: (positive) communion, revelation, priest; (negative) sorrow

Brown: (positive) humility, compassion; (negative) compromise, humanism

Gold: (positive) purity, glory, prosperity, wisdom, durability; (negative) idolatry, defilement, contamination, lawlessness

Gray: (positive) maturity, honor; (negative) death, sadness, weakness

Green: (positive) growth, prosperity, life; (negative) greed, envy, pride

Orange: (positive) perseverance, vitality; (negative) stubborn, willful

Pink: (positive) childlike love or faith; (negative) childish, immature

Purple: (positive) royalty, kingship; (negative) false authority, oppression

Red: (positive) blood atonement, sacrifice, power; (negative) anger, war

Silver: (positive) redemption; (negative) temptation, covetousness

White: (positive) purity, holy power/Spirit; (negative) legalistic spirit

Yellow: (positive) hope, strength, gifts from God; (negative) coward, fear

DIRECTIONS

East: beginning, law, God's manifest presence entering

North: (positive) God's throne, Heaven, authority; (negative) judgment

South: (positive) seeking truth; (negative) fleshly, sin, corruption

West: end, death, last, grace, related to the tabernacle

Left: rejected, condemned, human weakness

Left Turn: spiritual change

Right: accepted, rewarded by God, authority, favor, power, the strength of man or power of God revealed in man

Right Turn: natural change

Back: previous event or experience, past sins, sins of forefathers, unaware, ambush, hidden, memory

Front: future, prophecy, immediate or "at your front door"

FOOD

Apples: spiritual fruit, temptation, something precious

Bread: Jesus Christ, Word of God, God's provision

Corn: blessings of God

Eggs: promise of God, prayers yet to be fulfilled

Fig Leaves: self-atonement, man-made covering

Fruit: spiritual fruitfulness (note amount, size, color, freshness)

Grapes: fruitfulness, success in life, connected to Christ

Honey: sweet, strength, wisdom, abundance

Lemons: sour, a poor sport

Manna: miraculous provision, bread of life

Meat: spiritually maturity, depth in God's Word

Milk: Good nourishment, elementary teaching, immaturity

Orange: (positive) perseverance, power, energy; (negative) danger

Pears: long life, enduring much without complaining

Pumpkin: witchcraft, deception, snare, trick

Strawberries: goodness, virtuous, healing, sweet, humble

Tomato: kindness, big hearted, heart of God, generous

Water: Holy Spirit, refreshing, Word of God

Wine: (positive) outpouring of the Spirit; (negative) drunkenness

INSECTS

Ant: (positive) diligence, wise; (negative) insignificant

Bee/Hornet: painful, strong demonic attack or power

Butterfly: (positive) freedom, fragile, transformation; (negative) flighty

Flies: evil spirits; filth of hell, the occult

Grasshopper: destruction

Moth: symbol of destruction

Roach: infestation, unclean spirits, hidden sin

Scorpion: evil spirits, evil people, painful attack

Spider: occultic attack, witchcraft

METALS

Brass: judgment
Bronze: strength
Gold: divine nature of God
Iron: bondage
Lead: weight of sin, wickedness, foolishness
Silver: redemption, wisdom
Tin: dross, waste, worthless, cheap, putrification

Miscellaneous

Blanket: covering someone else's sin, hiding

Brick: slavery, human effort

Bridle: restraint, control

Candle: Holy Spirit, light, revelation

Clouds: divine presence, covering

Crown: authority, Jesus, to reign, honored, rewarded

Cup: life, health

Cymbal: vibration, praise, worship

Dreaming: message within a message, vision

Drowning: overcome, self-pity, depression, grief, debt

Falling: unsupported, trials, backsliding

Feathers: covering, protection

Flying: call to move in the higher things of God

Gate: spiritual authority, entrance point for good/evil

Key: spiritual authority, unveiling secrets, lock or unlock

Kiss: covenant, enticement, deception, betrayal

Ladder: Christ connecting Heaven and earth, ability to ascend something

Life Seasons: may include former places you have been or lived, former schools, tests, or jobs; assess what was significant about that season of your life

Mirror: (positive) looking at yourself or your heart, looking back, past; (negative) vanity, self-centeredness

Miscarriage: to lose something at the preparatory stage, whether good or bad, plans aborted

Money: gain or loss of favor, greed

Check: favor

Credit Card: attempting to walk in something you don't have yet, debt, lack of trust

Moon: light in darkness, Son of Man, reflecting God's glory

Nail: security, establish

Oil: Holy Spirit, anointing

Pen: tongue, indelible words, record, covenant, agreement

Pencil: agreement that could change or be erased

Pillar: strength, steadfastness, assistance

Plow: breaking new ground

Pregnancy: in process of reproducing, preparatory stage, the promise of God, the Word of God as seed, prophetic word, desire, anticipation, expectancy, filled with the purposes of God that are preparing to come forth

Repeating Activities: God establishing a matter or issue, repeating because you are not listening, take notice

Refrigerator: preservation, keeping something fresh for future use

Television: (positive) spiritual sight and understanding; (negative) entertainment, fleshly cravings and desires, dull spirit

Nature and Weather

Beach: waiting for the return of Christ

Looking Out at Water: waiting for something

Walking Along Beach or Sunning Self: tranquility

Blizzard: inability to see, storm blinding you to something

Desert: temptation, desolation, solitude

Earthquake: judgment or shaking

Fire: presence of God, purifying, testing

Flood: (positive) overflowing of goodness; (negative) judgment of sin

Flower: fading human glory, frailty, delicate

Lilies: beauty, majesty

Rose: Christ and His church

Garden: growth, fertility

Grass: frailty of flesh

Mountain: (positive) place of prayer, Heaven, refuge, place of meeting with God; (negative) impossibility or obstacles

Rain: blessing, cleansing, dirty rain is from enemy

Rainbow: promise of God

River: River of Life, presence of God, move of the Holy Spirit, coming into your Promised Land

Snow: blessing, refreshing, righteousness, purity

Storms: light in color can be from God, dark can be trouble from the enemy, turbulent times, judgment

Stream: living water, refreshment

Tidal Wave: great move of Holy Spirit, revival, judgment

Tornadoes: winds of change (negative or positive depending on color of tornado), destructive times coming, judgment, drastic change, danger

Valley: dark night of the soul, hopelessness, sadness, time when God seems silent, low time emotionally, place of decision, place of hiddenness with God

Waves: tumultuous people or stormy season, false doctrine

Wind: (positive) Holy Spirit; (negative) adversity

Numbers*

1: unity, superiority, priority, beginnings, God Himself

2: faithful witness, set apart, manifest power, godly division

3: perfect completion, fullness, resurrection, divinity

4: creation, things made, the "world"

5: grace, overcoming

6: flesh of man, satan

7: Spirit of God, perfection, completion

8: new beginnings

9: (positive) fruit bearing and life; (negative) judgment and death

10: perfect order, timelines and carrying out God's plan

11: (positive) heroes rising, selfless service; (negative) disorder

12: perfect government, God is in control, apostolic

13: rebellion, backsliding

14: generational promises, fear of the Lord, witness of Him

15: rest, overcoming death, perfect grace (3x5)

16: love of God

17: overcoming victory

18: (positive) life more abundant; (negative) bondage of sin (3x6)

19: faith

20: waiting, expectancy

30: blood of Jesus, beginning of ministry

111: the Trinity, God Himself

222: signs, miracles, and wonders

333: God calling you or revealing great and mighty things

444: complete creation, the whole world

555: complete grace, Christ Himself

666: full or complete lawlessness, fully flesh

777: perfection of spirit

888: resurrection, new beginnings, Jesus

10,000: maturity

*From my book *Numbers That Preach*

PEOPLE

Baby: new life, new Christian, new ministry or responsibility, new beginning, dependent and helpless, innocent

Bride: Christ's church, covenant or relationship

Carpenter: Jesus, building or fixing, preacher

Faceless Person: angelic being or Holy Spirit (Note color: dark color, demonic; light color, heavenly)

Father: authority, God, author, originator, source, inheritance

Giant: (positive) Godly person of spiritual stature, strong in the Lord, a conqueror; (negative) demon, defilement

Harlot/Prostitute: a tempting situation, flesh, worldly, demon

Hijacker: (positive) God taking control; (negative) enemy wanting to take control of you or a situation

Lawyer: (positive) Jesus Christ (our Advocate), mediator; (negative) the accuser; satan, legalism

Mob: false accusation

Policeman: authority for good or evil, protector, spiritual authority

Prisoner: a lost soul; addiction

Shepherd: Jesus Christ, God; leader, good or bad, selfless person, protector

Twins: (positive) double blessing and anointing; (negative) double trouble

ROOMS IN A HOUSE

Attic: history, past issues, family history

Basement: (positive) foundation, basics; (negative) hidden issues

Bathroom: place of cleansing; spiritual toxins removed

Bathroom in Full View: humbling season

Bedroom: intimacy, rest

Dining Room/Eating: partaking of spiritual food, fellowship

Kitchen: preparing spiritual food, teaching ministry

Living Room: family life, fellowship, how you are living

Transportation

Airplane: prophetic gifting

Armored Car: protection of God

Automobile: personal ministry, your destiny or life

Bicycle: messenger, individual ministry, hard work

Bus: church or ministry

Chariot: major spiritual encounter

Coal Car: on track, work being directed by the Lord

Combine/Harvester: evangelism, harvest of souls

Convertible: open heaven in your ministry, job or life

Fire Truck: rescue ministry, putting out fires

Fred Flintstone Car: human effort

Hang Glider: being driven by the wind of the Spirit

Helicopter: mobile and flexible

Limousine: (positive) taken to destiny in style; (negative) materialism

Mini Van: family

Motorcycle: fast, powerful, maneuverable

Moving Van: transition, change

Roller Coaster: exciting, but could lead to destruction

Sailboat: powered by wind of the Spirit

Semitruck: transporting large amounts

Speedboat: fast, exciting, power in the Spirit

Submarine: undercover and active, hidden ministry

Subway: undercover and active, underground ministry

Taxi Cab: hireling, paying the price to get somewhere

Tow Truck: ministry of helps, gathering the wounded

Tractor: need to plow hard ground or sow seed

Train: great momentum, force or following

Truck: ability to transport or deliver

Tugboat: providing assistance, ministry of helps

TREES

Trees: (depending on size and type) leaders, mature believers, steady, firmly rooted, nation or national leader

Cedar: royalty

Evergreen: long life, always fruitful and beautiful

Fig: Israel

Forest: symbol of the nations

Mulberry: spiritual warfare

Myrtle: prosperity and abundance

Oak: strength

Palm: praise and worship

WEAPONS

Arrow: (positive) children; (negative) accusation from the enemy

Dart: (positive) accuracy; (negative) curses, demonic attack

Gun: spiritual authority good or bad, spiritual attack

Knife: (positive) if in your hand, protection; (negative) brutal attack, gossip

Shield: faith, protection, God's truth

Sword: Word of God, further reaching, authority

ABOUT THE AUTHOR

Troy A. Brewer, the senior pastor of OpenDoor Church in Burleson, Texas, is renowned for his prophetic insights and teachings that simplify complex Kingdom principles. He is the author of 16 influential books, including bestsellers like *Numbers That Preach, Redeeming Your Timeline,* and *Looking Up,* along with many study guides, reference guides and numerous additional resources. His teachings are broadcast globally through *The OpenDoor Experience* on networks such as Daystar and GOD TV. Aside from his ministry work, Troy is a passionate abolitionist and founder of Troy Brewer Ministries, which is directly responsible for the rescue of over 11,000 women and children from sex trafficking, providing them with essential care and a path to transformation through King Jesus. Through his efforts and partnerships, including SPARK Worldwide, founded by Troy's wife, Pastor Leanna Brewer, there are over 4,000 children under their care to date. Troy continues to impact lives worldwide through his various platforms, including his on-demand and live-streaming service, odx.tv, and prophetic mentorship podcast, PULSE 24.

From

Troy A. Brewer

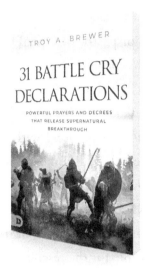

TROY A. BREWER

31 BATTLE CRY DECLARATIONS

POWERFUL PRAYERS AND DECREES
THAT RELEASE SUPERNATURAL
BREAKTHROUGH

YOUR SPIRITUAL ARSENAL AWAITS WITHIN.
ARE YOU READY TO CLAIM IT?

When battles rage against the forces of darkness, you need more than mere faith—you need weapons. Weapons forged in holy fire, to pierce the heart of darkness and dispel the oppressive forces that seek to stifle your soul.

Troy Brewer, renowned pastor, minister, and prophet, hands you the very tools of the trade. With 31 potent and practical declarations, he equips you to not just stand your ground, but reclaim it. Every word, every decree, rooted deeply in the victory of the cross, serves as both shield and sword against the onslaught of demonic assignments.

Troy's challenge to you is clear: Don't just witness the power of the cross. Wield it. Become a conqueror, reverse the tide from loss to victory, and emerge not just a believer, but a spiritual conqueror.

Purchase your copy wherever books are sold

From
Troy A. Brewer

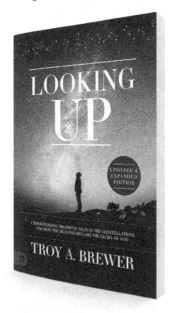

Signs in the Heavens

Until the mid-20th century, the heavens were the greatest show on Earth. Ancient people recognized the same constellations we do today, though they understood the signs behind those pictures in the sky in a way that's been lost to us – until now.

Troy Brewer reveals the connection between the story in the stars and the Biblical account of the fall of man and redemption through Jesus.

What does the night sky tell us about God's plan? How does the Almighty speak through the constellations?

The answers are astounding as the dramatic truth about the cosmos is unveiled for these last days. The time is short. We should all be *Looking Up*.

Purchase your copy wherever books are sold

From

Troy A. Brewer

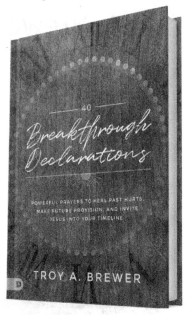

Powerful prayers and declarations that supernaturally redeem your past and miraculously prepare your future

In his bestselling book *Redeeming Your Timeline*, pastor and author, Troy Brewer showed you the radical transformation that is possible when you invite God into your personal history and timeline.

Now, in *40 Breakthrough Declarations*, Troy equips you with practical tools to reverse the plans of the enemy, release Heaven's healing power, and exchange the pain of your past for a glorious future filled with hope and purpose!

This powerful book features compelling devotionals and specific declarations to...

- Identify and break strongholds that hinder personal progress.
- Speak words that dismantle the enemy's lies.
- Experience divine reversals of hurt, shame, and pain as you apply Jesus' redemption to your past, present, and future.
- Prophesy hope and healing to places of trauma.

The Lord wants to bring redemption into every situation in your life, and He wants to partner with you to do it. Learn to speak the words that release His power over your timeline!

Purchase your copy wherever books are sold

Check out
our **Destiny Image**
bestsellers page at
destinyimage.com/bestsellers

for cutting-edge,
prophetic messages
that will supernaturally
empower you and the
body of Christ.

From
Rick Renner

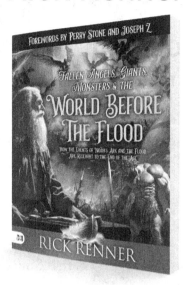

Do You Have Questions About the World Before the Flood?
Does the Bible Really Explain the 'Unexplainable'?

In this book, Rick Renner — historian and Bible teacher with extensive knowledge of New Testament Greek — clears up some rampant erroneous theories while uncovering brand-new revelations from the Bible. He uses archaeological findings, the writings of Church fathers, trusted historical documents,and Scripture to answer these and other questions, such as:

- When was the first recorded rapture? What does it tell us about the rapture of the Church?
- Are the "sons of God" in Genesis and the fallen angels the same thing?
- Who were the watchers God assigned to guard mankind after the Fall?
- Was Methuselah's life a prophetic demonstration of God's longsuffering that preceded judgment?
- What did God's promise of "120 years" really mean?
- Where is Noah's Ark today? And why did God save only Noah and his family?
- Are there any consequences of unholy living today?

Using photos from his own expeditions in the lower Ararat mountains — along with other empirical evidence of the Ark's location — Rick captivates readers in this book *and brings the Bible to life* concerning this favorite childhood story. Containing hundreds of photos, illustrations, and endnotes, *Fallen Angels, Giants, Monsters, and the World Before the Flood* is "a museum in a book" and a must-have edition to refreshand refire your walk with God!

Purchase your copy wherever books are sold.

In the Right Hands, This Book Will Change Lives!

Most of the people who need this message will not be looking for this book. To change their lives, you need to **put a copy of this book in their hands.**

Our ministry is constantly seeking methods to find the people who need this anointed message to change their lives. **Will you help us reach these people?**

Extend this ministry by sowing three, five, ten, or *even more* books today and change people's lives for the better! Your generosity will be part of catalyzing the Great Awakening that many have been prophesying and praying for.

Made in the USA
Monee, IL
12 January 2025

76610728R00168